Massee's Guide to
EATING
AND DRINKING
IN EUROPE

Books by William E. Massee

MASSEE'S GUIDE TO
EATING AND DRINKING IN EUROPE

MASSEE'S WINE-FOOD INDEX

WINES AND SPIRITS
a complete buying guide

WINE HANDBOOK

WINES OF FRANCE
(in collaboration with Alexis Lichine)

THE ART OF COMFORT

Massee's Guide to EATING AND DRINKING IN EUROPE

By WILLIAM E. MASSEE

McGraw-Hill Book Company, Inc.

NEW YORK   TORONTO   LONDON

Library of Congress Catalog Card Number: 63-13937

First Edition

40692

For Cathy
who tries everything once

CONTENTS

INTRODUCTION

This book could be called a *Freeloader's Guide to Europe*, because it lists hundreds of places where you can get free booze—Scotch, Irish, Cognac, brandies and liqueurs, wines and beers—and everything else from soup to nuts. What could be better for an eager tourist? But it didn't start out like that, and I don't think it ends up like that, either.

A country's food and drink—how it's made, what it's like, and how good it is—is the surest and fastest guide to finding out about a land and its people. A sidewalk café in Paris, a Munich beer hall, an Irish pub, a Viennese *wurstl* stand, a taffy barrow in Florence, a fish-and-chips in London, an Amsterdam herring cart, a Danish *smørrebrød*, a Zurich bakery, a Spanish *bodega*, a Norwegian fishmarket, a Swedish grocery—all make us part of Europe. And the tastes—our best memory apparatus—make Europe ours.

Eating and drinking encompass all the common, homely arts and skills of a time and place, repeated over and over again, every day. They make us conscious of where we are, right now, this moment—of that state the French call, sharply, *constatation*. The object is to put ourselves where this can happen most excitingly, where we can expand our being and our knowing. Some of the happenings are so common and so natural we scarcely notice, like the oven-dried bread set on the table with the silver in any good London club, or the golden, crystal sugar, or the broad beans served with the roast. And that's in London, where everybody knows nobody cares for food, for eating is not really nice!

Americans are lucky because everything's strange, so they are often conscious of what's there, and have the chance to be particularly aware of and sensitive to these essences revealed. Such things mark distinctions and make true differences and point out real samenesses. A cookie factory or a distillery is as revealing as a dam or a plant making computers. And it's more interesting. And it's easier to understand.

"What's the name of a winery in Burgundy I can go to, and what are some restaurants I shouldn't miss? Should I bother going to the Moselle? And what about Dublin? I haven't got much time, and even less money, so is the Tour d'Argent really worth it?"

Americans are wildly curious about the good things to eat and drink in Europe, not because ours at home are so bad but because some of it is now so good. People naturally want more and more and more, after growing up in a supermarket society where things for so long kept getting worse and worse and worse. We are just beginning to enjoy our abundance and take advantage of it. There is still the steak-and-chicken tourist, but he is swallowed up in the palace hotels and international restaurants, the same everywhere, like stops on a thruway. We have developed shunpike tours now, and palace-poopers and scoffmaws unmoved by restaurant French and fancy type.

It's what's on the plate that counts, and the plate damned well better be hot.

We take our timidities to Europe, and our self-consciousness, and our reluctance to try strange things or to make a fuss. But we take our curiosity, too, and our appetites. We spend hundreds of dollars to get there, the precious holidays, and we're looking for things we can't get in Cleveland or New York or San Francisco. This isn't the same as the old search for identity, or an escape to something foreign. We just want to know what's going on in the world we are trying to live in.

It's quite a shock. Europe is beginning to find out about the supermarket society. Americans know all about the trash and king-size cartons that come with abundance; Europeans don't know what's hitting them. The Common Market is working fine, but lots of Europeans are still doubting if it can get going at all, unable to see what's happening before their eyes. More and more palace hotels and international restaurants are being built, but they are filling up with Europeans now, not just Americans.

The specialties are disappearing, the street markets are disappearing. The egg laid this morning is a rarity, replaced by the one laid last week, in another country. The butter comes from storage, not straight from the churn, the vegetables are being raised for appearance not for taste. The food packers talk about shelf life and turnover and impulse positions and packaging, not about freshness and ripeness and top quality.

Oh, it's all just beginning, but it's there. Snack bars everywhere, quick service, soda pop. The American experience is that there is always a place for quality at a profit in any market, no matter how large or how small, if you are willing to solve all the problems involved. Europeans don't seem to be learning from that American experience.

They aren't helped to understanding by the Americans who still order steak and chicken and Martinis, but they don't learn from the others, either.

Europe's a big place now, 220 million in the Common Market, 90 million in the Outer Seven, and still quite a few people to be heard from. Before a lot of it goes down the drain, tourists have a chance to try the country specialties, to taste dishes carefully prepared out of the best materials, to find the owner-chef who's more interested in how you like it than in what you pay for it. People have been complaining about the declining European cuisine for generations now. Balzac was so appalled he wrote a dictionary of cuisine so at least a record would remain. A lot of it is going to stay, and maybe Europe will learn the trick of having quantity and quality at the same time. But prices are going up, recipes are being simplified, staffs are being reduced, menus are being internationalized, and mustard now comes in tubes, like toothpaste. That doesn't matter, it's still the same old mustard, but there's a question of making it smoother by adding a little oil, and there's a chemical—doesn't affect the taste hardly at all—that keeps it from turning brown. . . .

This book is intended to save the traveler time—not just hours but weeks. It is supposed to take away his fear of trying new dishes with strange names, or at least make him feel so at ease that he will ask questions and find out what's on the menu, before settling for an omelet or a steak. It is meant to suggest that the out-of-the-way, the side street, the shabby, even the dirty hole-in-the-wall, may be more exciting than a restaurant duly noted in a travel guide. After all, no American goes abroad without bismuth and paregoric, and what else is there to worry about? Just leave the cash and the extra traveler's checks in the hotel.

I've always envied the American going abroad for the first time, innocent as a babe, on a foreign strand. I never had it so good. We were met at the boat by my brother and his wife, and were led around by the nose for weeks until we got used to it all. No chance to find out on our own, which is the most exciting way, full of confusion, doubt, fear. Then somebody grins at you and everything's fine. If we'd just had a book that told us how to order a beer, something that listed the things we ought to try. . . .

This last time I found out that it's impolite in France to let the bottle touch the glass when you're pouring. Really upsetting. Now that's a little bit of cultural shock I've been submitting my French friends to for years, never knowing I was upsetting them. I should have known. It's the simple things one misses.

Travel is best when you are in love, and your lover is with you. That gives you courage, and the chance to try two things on the menu. If one of them doesn't turn out, everything isn't lost. Without a lover, traveling is best when you are in love with something, because it's hard to see clearly when you are frightened and turned inwards. The best thing to be in love with is what happens every day. Part of this is food and drink, which is comforting and companionable. This book is supposed to be a comfort.

I remember our first day in France, a dozen years ago. My wife was with our first child, to be born months later in Paris, and we were happy to be in a place we'd wanted to see for so long. It was the day before the season opened in Deauville, but one of the restaurants agreed to feed us. We had mussels—marvelous, the essence of the sea—which we had never tasted before, and then we had a lousy, tough steak and soggy French fries. Our bliss was broken, and we walked along the street gloomily, on our way to bed. A bright coffeeshop was open and we went in. Nobody else was there. The owner said he had some wood strawberries that had just come in from the farm, brought in with the cream. We had them, and cups of coffee, and little glasses of green Chartreuse. My wife burst into tears.

"What's the matter?" I said. "What's the matter?"

"Everything tastes so good," she said.

I don't suppose I'd make the point clearer by describing the strawberries and cream. But we've remembered them for a long time. We have lots of such memories. This book is intended to make them easier to come by.

FRANCE

GASTRONOMY. Many regional stews and pot dishes go back to Roman times, but French cuisine as we know it was developed from Italian dishes brought to the court of Louis XIV. French sauce cookery became world-wide, but the French preserved many of their local dishes, as varied as the countryside, built around butter in the north, fat in the mountains and the middle, oil and garlic and tomatoes in the south. There is an ancient tradition of producing excellent raw materials, and the simple cooking of these is the glory of French cooking. More than any other nation the French honor good food, and have developed all the arts of the table—table-setting, service, presentation—so that their ideals have become the standard.

BREAKFAST. *Café au lait*, strong coffee and hot milk, with bread or rolls, particularly buttery *croissants* and rich *brioches*, with jam, are customary. Tea and chocolate, English breakfasts, fruits and juices, are available in most hotels.

LUNCH & DINNER. Lunch can be bread, cheese, and wine, an omelet, a sausage, or fish, although grilled meats and stews are found on most menus. Dinner usually consists of an appetizer and soup, an entree of

7

fish or sea food, and a main course of meat or fowl, followed by cheese and dessert. Wines are customary with both meals.

STREET FOOD.   A sandwich is usually ham in a roll, but there are many modern snack bars, teashops, and pastry shops. Stalls sell oysters, carts sell ice cream, and the local *charcuterie* sells all kinds of delicatessen.

PARIS

The first thing to do in Paris is to get settled. Then go out to a café. The adventure begins.

What to order! *Un demi de blonde*—light French beer is wonderful; *un citron pressé*—lemonade squeezed from fresh lemons; *un Perrier*—soda water with a slice of lemon floating in its sparkle; *un bon café*—the *café ordinaire* can be terrible; *une fine à l'eau*—Cognac with a splash and ice is fine when you're excited; *un chocolat chaud*—two pitchers both hot, one of cocoa syrup and the other milk; *un Pernod avec de la glace*, or maybe *un Ricard*—like absinthe and very quenching with water and ice; *un Dubonnet* or maybe *une Suze*—nothing like an *apéritif* with ice to make you feel at home.

Where to eat! *Haute cuisine* in a starred restaurant? Quenelles are melting fish dumplings in a sauce; or maybe *écrevisses*, for crayfish are one of the finest dishes of French cuisine; or *alose* or *sole* or *truite*, because shad, sole, and trout are unmatched; maybe Belons or Marennes because oysters are particularly fine and not fatty; then there's *pâté en croute*, a sort of glorified meat loaf; or a *petite marmite* or *potage St.-Germain*, because a strong bouillon or creamy pea soup would be good to start with. That's the first course. Also the second, if we try two things.

To follow? There's the pressed duck or the *poulet de Bresse*—I can't describe them, you have to taste them. We could have *pommes de terre soufflées* with either, or *dauphines*, the first all puffed up, the second crusty pillows of whipped potatoes—these, too, you'll have to taste to find out how good they are. For dessert, a tart or soufflé. If we have two courses to start with, maybe we should have veal—no, red meat would be better, and a cheese course before the dessert to be sure we'll be able to finish the red wine. I think a Bordeaux would be lighter than a Burgundy, don't you?

But perhaps we should start with a simpler meal from *la bonne cuisine*, in a place that serves dishes out of *Tante Marie*—what's called home cooking, or *la cuisine bourgeoise*. How about *bœuf bouilli* or *escalope de veau* or *gigot rôti*—boiled beef, veal scallops, or roast lamb done the French way. Or maybe even better would be the old dishes from the provinces, *la cuisine régionale;* we could go to a *brasserie*—the word means brewery in French but refers to a café that specializes in beer and usually Alsatian food—for some *jambon de York* or a *choucroute garnie*, which is sauerkraut with ham and smoked pork and the sausages called cervelat, with peppercorns and juniper in the *choucroute*. Or maybe we should go to a wine restaurant and have a *ragoût*—you can't beat stew—a green salad, and some cheeses, *Carré de l'est* or *Pont l'Évêque*.

Hard to decide. *Haute cuisine* is Paris food, a repertoire of dishes built up from the materials and ancient recipes of the île de France, with a few tossed in from *la bonne cuisine* for good measure. Chefs scoured the country to please the court, and the result is a sort of notation for exceptional dishes that can be prepared by any chef who's learned his basic sauces and techniques. The cooks were pulled around the world, their sauces masking all sorts of poor materials and preparation. The names are the same in New York or New Delhi, Toronto or Vienna, but they rarely taste the way they do in Paris, because the materials are different. Tourists trained to know the names rarely know the taste of the dishes because they vary so widely from one resort or palace hotel to another.

Haute cuisine follows two paths of higher sophistication. One of these is toward what might be called *la grande cuisine*, the elaborate and often architectural preparation of *pièces montées*, in which the rare, the expensive, and the overrefined are manifest. Tiny but very rich dishes, fantastic garnishes, painstaking delicacies, delicious frivolities, almost too elegant and luxurious for weak mortals in an imperfect world. Sometimes they taste awful, too.

The other direction of *haute cuisine* is toward bringing out the essence of perfect materials in the simplest way, so that the result is perfection, one matchless course following another, the dinner and the evening and the companions becoming the very thing that life is all about, a time of joy and peace and wonder. I have seen people cry, everything was so good, a sophisticated chef blush like a twelve-year-old when praised by a happy crowd who realized what he'd done, an owner present to the happy guests the last bottle of a brandy laid down by his grandfather. I've seen other guests applaud a table of diners who were enjoying well and so enthusiastically that they had become tipsy with perfection. In France, there are three chances for this to happen every day, but if it actually occurs two or three times a year, you are blessed.

Such cooking is back in the direction of *la bonne cuisine*. It might be called *la cuisine simple*. This is the absolute height of French cooking, and depends entirely on the skill of the chef, on his genius and his courage.

A great cook cannot have too big a restaurant, because he will not then be able to supervise everything himself. He can't have too large a menu, because he does not have enough hours in a day to prepare many dishes, let alone complicated ones that may require much attention. He must have time to buy the perfect materials, and they must be available to him promptly enough so that they will be at their peak. He must have customers wise enough to understand what he is preparing, rich enough to be able to afford it, and generous enough to praise, because chefs need admiration as much as they need pots. The three-starred restaurants in Michelin, and many of the two-starred restaurants throughout France, are supposed to approach this level of perfection. There are endless arguments as to how many of them do, and each diner must be his own judge.

Restaurants serving *la bonne cuisine*, not so elaborate dishes that still require skill and good materials in their preparation, with the touch of a born cook to raise them above the level of excellence, used to abound in France. Many of them are left. But cooking is such hard work, hours are so long, diners are so hurried and unknowing, and there are so many easier ways to make a living. More and more, people demand fancy foods, or familiar ones, passing up a stew for veal in a fancy sauce, ordering

steaks or chops instead of the *pot-au-feu* or *cassoulet*, so
that many of the common dishes are taken off the menu,
taking the heart out of the cook, as well. It's like the
mother who bursts into tears after she has spent all afternoon preparing something wonderful, and then sees it
all disappear in ten minutes, the family saying, boy that's
good, can we be excused? Artists hate failure but they
hate lack of appreciation much more. How sad it is. We
must cheer up.

Many recipes from the good family cooking pass over
into the *haute cuisine* and purists get all upset. What's
blanquette de veau doing on the menu of a great Paris
restaurant? they'll say; that isn't elegant. But the nature
of the repertoire is to grow as new materials appear, and
the good chef is constantly experimenting with new combinations, or refining or adapting traditional and foreign
recipes. The puffy fried potatoes called *pommes soufflées*
came into being, it is said, because a celebrity was late to
a dedicatory lunch, and the cook had to plunge them a
second time into the hot fat. Chicken Marengo was a
whip-up dish for Napoleon, just before the battle in
which he defeated the Austrians in 1800. *Pêche Melba*
and countless other dishes have been devised by chefs in
honor of special guests and famous occasions. Most often,
the basic idea of the dish goes back to *la bonne cuisine*.

French regional dishes which come to Paris menus also
turn outward for inspiration, busily adapting or adopting
whenever the prospects glitter. Alsatian dishes borrow
heavily from the Germans; Provence and Riviera cooking turns to Italy and the eastern Mediterranean; Basque
dishes show the influence of Spain and the Moors; Flanders
looks to Belgium. It's always a pleasure to lurk around

the borders in France for a few days before moving on, regaled with the gustatory ruffles and flourishes that come in a different form once you pass the barriers.

Cooking is called the ninth art in France, and remains a living tradition. But it's no longer true that you can walk into any French restaurant and get a good meal. It probably never was. There was once so much good cooking that it seemed that way. Only a few years ago, travelers looked for the signs marking the *routiers*, truck driver stops where the food was hearty, simple and good. Few good ones are left. More and more is going into showmanship, less and less into the kitchen. The young people turn their backs on the *grand gourmet* tradition of their fathers, if only to protect against any characteristic of the empty world left to them. In a decade most of the classic cuisine and its epicurean admirers may be gone, many people say. It survives, like the theater, in spite of constant doom-preaching since the days of the Revolution. But wise travelers seek it out today, just in case. Anyway, life is short, so while there's still appetite, places to satisfy it, and companions to enjoy it with, Paris kitchens are there to excite you.

Les Halles is the place to go to see how the miracle of Paris food occurs each day. Here, the restaurants and hotels buy their supplies. The market is as much a Paris monument as Notre Dame or the Eiffel Tower, perhaps even closer to the heart and soul of Paris, which must certainly be good food and drink. Travelers today pass up monuments, forsaking past for present, fearful of their own innocence, but Les Halles, like the eating places of Paris, the food shops, the cafés, is a monument of the moment, of the next few minutes, of dinner tonight, as pleasurable as a moment in the kitchen while things are cooking. Hope in France is not a feeling for a future dream, over the rainbow, but anticipation of what's for supper, what's coming up next. Anticipation rises high at Les Halles, beginning shortly after midnight, when the trucks come in from the country, already dwindling at dawn. It is surrounded with bistros—a stand-up bar, made of and called a *zinc*, a few tables, five or six dishes chalked on a blackboard, where a bowl of onion soup carries Americans back to the twenties. Heaps of vegetables and fruits and flowers—the smells, the bustle, the morning sun—all show what a fine day it's going to be. Les Halles is due to be torn down in 1966, so not much time to see it is left.

Among the categories of eating places listed by Michelin are those of *grande classe, élégance Parisienne, confort cossu* (which means solid comfort), *classiques, choisis et variés, atmosphère originale, grands cafés élégants, cuisines specialisées,* and half a dozen more. It is the best guide in all the world, and no traveler in France with an interest in food or curious about where to eat would travel without it. The guides for Spain, Italy and other countries are equally reliable and impartial. There is an over-all one for France that lists at least one restaurant of worth in every town of any size, including the specialties if the restaurant deserves a star. For Paris and each of the regions there are special guides that go into detail about local joys.

A word about the restaurant classification in Michelin, which is a model of compactness. Crossed spoons and forks indicate price, four pairs indicating very expensive, three warning that it will be expensive, two showing that it is not cheap, and one indicating that it is not expensive. The forks are supposed to indicate that prices are reasonable for what you get, and usually do so. In Paris, a dinner of two or three courses and a bottle of wine, plus dessert, might cost twenty dollars a person in a four-fork restaurant, perhaps five dollars less in the country. A not unsafe rule of thumb is to allow five dollars per person for each symbol in Paris, and four dollars in the country. Some de luxe restaurants warrant five marks of crossed silver, and you ought to try at least one of these while you're in Paris; others have no crossed silver, and you ought to try a lot of these.

The stars are most important. There are scarcely a dozen that warrant three stars in all of France, and the constellation means the house warrants a special journey —*vaut le voyage*. The number of such restaurants changes from year to year, the loss of a star causing despair, the gaining of one great rejoicing. Two stars indicate a restaurant worth going out of your way to get to (*mérite un détour*), and a single star indicates a fine place in the district—*une bonne table dans la localité*. Americans are pumped so full of superlatives from birth that they have a tendency to ignore the one- and two-star restaurants, as being just a little better than ordinary and more expensive. Not at all.

A one-star restaurant is what we'd say is one of the best in town, and a two-star restaurant we'd be apt to call absolutely out of this world. And the price is shown by the crossed silver. As for three-star restaurants, we have no equivalent. In all of the United States there may be three or four restaurants that warrant three stars, and at least two of them would be in New York. All of them would have five or six pairs of crossed silver.

I don't mean to take a slap at American restaurants. We have good chefs and good materials everywhere, but our restaurants are more expensive to operate and to decorate, and few people could afford or would want to pay for what a three-star meal would cost in just about any city in America. We have many that match French two-star restaurants, but they are very expensive.

A star in the country is worth two in Paris, the saying goes, and perhaps it was once true. Everybody complains about how Paris food has declined, meaning that the starred restaurants are now all expensive and crowded, and that the average restaurant isn't as good as it used to be. The fact is probably that a lot of mediocre restaurants have appeared to take care of tourists and young people who don't care that much about food. There are more and more self-service places, cafeterias, *les quicks*, where you can get a sandwich; there's an American drugstore of sorts on the Champs-Élysées that's one of the most popular places in Paris among the Parisians, who love novelty.

The best way to get to know the pleasures of eating in Paris is to settle down in one part of town for a few weeks and try the various places in the *quartier*. If you're lucky enough to have an apartment, there's the pleasure of shopping in the local market, of buying delicatessen from the local *charcuterie*, fresh bread twice a day from the *boulangerie*, cakes and pastry from the *patisseries*, and the rest. It's a way to get to know the people, and to learn a lot about a way of life that singles out for consideration many things we are apt to take for granted, don't know about, or have forgotten: fresh bread warm from the oven, the first vegetables and fruits of a new season, a special shipment of fish, the Christmas cakes and Easter logs, a well-larded roast, *oursins* (sea urchins) in the street stalls, crescents of coconut in the nickel fountains.

Before you leave, there are certain culinary monuments to shop in: Corcellet's near l'Opéra for groceries, where they have a collection of singing coffeepots; Dehillerin near Les Halles, for kitchen equipment; nearby Battendier for *charcuterie;* Fauchon's and Hédiard's, both on Place de la Madeleine, for delicacies; nearby Maison de la Truffe for truffles; Androuet's for cheeses; in Neuilly there's Bezançon's for all kinds of ice cream, and there are the big stores of Félix Potin for groceries, and Nikolas for wines. Sabatier has knives, the Bazar de l'Hôtel de Ville as well as the department stores has all sorts of household supplies, and behind it is the section where you can find those knickknacks of junk and luxury called *bibeloterie* and known as *les articles de Paris.*

There's one kind of restaurant not to miss in Paris, especially if you're going to the wine country. This is the kind that serves *vins du pays,* country wines that never used to be shipped overseas. There are lots of them, and the English call them Beaujolais bistros; people in London's wine and food trade keep lists of Paris restaurants in their pockets, constantly updating them, absolutely convinced the selections are better than those in Michelin.

For what it's worth, here is a London wine merchant's list of Beaujolais bistros: Chez l'Ami Louis, l'Ours Martin, Moulin-à-Vent, La Boule d'Or, Chope Danton, and La

Grille, near Les Halles. Then there's Au Roy Gourmet, Chez Marius, Allard, and Chez Joséphine.

Others on the wine merchant's list included the restaurant at 3 Rue Beauchaumont, the Brasserie Stella, Aux Crus de Bourgogne, Restaurant d'Artois, Marronniers, Le Cabaret, Grand Comptoir, St.-Jean Pied de Porc, and Le Santenay. He also said that he'd found a restaurant better than Alexandre Dumain's in Saulieu. It's the Hôtel de la Gare, in Montbard, about seventy miles southwest of Auxerre on Route 5. But Michelin only gives it two stars. Whom are you going to believe? Of course, if you're leaving Paris, it may not be *vaut le voyage*, but even Michelin says it *mérite un détour*, and it's right on the way to Burgundy.

THE WINE COUNTRY

Once in Paris, it's hard to know which way to turn. It's all there, in the wines and cheeses, fruits and berries, fish and sea food, meats and vegetables, each bearing the name of where it comes from. No need to go anywhere, except back for more, and how do you choose?

Well. *Vieille France* is the valley of the Loire, south of Paris. People still live in homes dug back into the valley hills, as they did thousands of years ago. The châteaux mark it as the vale of kings. Orléannais has the best game in France and is famed for its peasant cooking. The Touraine is called the garden of France, and has its pots of *rillettes*, a dice of pork and bacon to be spread on bread, unmatched with Vouvray to drink; there's Chinon, where Rabelais throve, and the vineyards of St.-Nicholas-de-Bourgueuil, and Tours itself, where shad and carp and barbel are supreme. There's Anjou, where a half bottle of wine is called a *fillette*, and the districts include those from slopes (called *coteaux*)—Saumur, Layon, La Loire and Le Loir—producing the Quart de Chaumes from Rochefort, the Coulée de Serrant from Savennières, and a hundred others. There are the Muscadet vineyards all around Nantes, near the river's mouth, and far upstream is the district of Pouilly-sur-Loire, which produces the fresh and delicious Pouilly-Fumé that's so good with *charcuterie*. In Vouvray, the vineyards are right above the caves dug in the hills, and some of the tasting rooms are a hundred feet below the ground. In Chinon the local hotel is called Gargantua, and you expect Rabelais to come in any minute for a *daube*, chunks of beef stewed in red Chinon, or duck stuffed with chestnuts and served with pickled walnuts. Perhaps there is no better place in the world for picnics, beside streams or the meandering river, a castle or vineyard on the slope, wine of the country cool from the stream, bread from the local *boulangerie*, plum tarts from the *patisserie*, and *charcuterie* that is certainly the best in the world, until you taste a better one tomorrow. If it isn't the most beautiful wine country in the world, it is certainly the most romantic, the most serene, the most enchanting. The Loire is for lovers and long afternoons. It is called the smile of France.

To the south and toward the coast is Cognac, the country that produces the most delicate brandies in all the world, and on the coast are the oyster beds, rated as to quality, that produce the Marennes, which are classed with the Whitstables and the Danish Limpfjord as the best in the world. Adjoining is Périgord, and the forests of Limousin, also rated into growths, or *crus*, that supply the only wood that's used for Cognac casks. Truffles, geese, and hogs come from Périgord, and here you can have truffles simmered in white wine, baked in the ashes, with eggs, combined with goose liver to make *pâté*, suckling pig stuffed with goose liver, bacon, and truffles, baked sweetbreads with truffles. And there's always Cognac to have afterwards.

The Cognac country is noted for the best butter in France, so there is much butter cookery there, as well as that with olive oil and fats. But a great deal of fish and sea food is eaten so meals will be light, leaving plenty of attention for the Cognac. You can try the various blends, the *Fine Champagne*, which is a blend of brandies distilled from the districts of Borderies, Fins Bois, and Bons Bois; and *Grande Fine Champagne*, from the districts of Grande Champagne and Petite Champagne. At the Cognac houses, you can taste the various brandies, and perhaps watch a blending. If you're lucky, you may be able to find a bottle of very old Cognac, perhaps twenty years or so, or even thirty. Brandies are usually bottled before they are that old because a longer time in cask makes them taste woody; many Cognacs reach good maturity at eight years, and others at twelve, but some stocks of very old brandies are kept for the blending. Once bottled, Cognac ceases to mature. "Napoléon" on a label no longer means much, except that the name is often reserved for the oldest Cognac marketed by a firm, 3-star being the name for the youngest.

South of Cognac is Bordeaux, the greatest wine region on earth. The big shippers are concentrated on the Quai des Chartrons, just off the town's main square. The great vineyards of the Médoc lie north of town, while those of

Graves begin in the suburbs to the south, with Sauternes below that. Many vineyards welcome visitors. But the most enchanting place is the district of St.-Émilion, across the river east of town, high on a bluff, a stopping point for those on pilgrimages to the shrines of Spain during the Middle Ages. Part of the town is at the foot of the bluff, including a hermit's cave with a pool in which you toss hairpins for luck, and a great chapel, still used for services. The tower of the chapel is up on the bluff at a corner of the town square. Also on the square is a restaurant with vine-covered terraces looking down to the river valley, and across to the vineyards. In and around the town are arches, columns, and bits of wall from the ancient city, and nearby are great caves once used for burial. There are few better places to have lunch on a summer day, and afterwards you can nibble unsweetened maca-roons that are a town specialty, as you finish the wine.

Still further south is the Armagnac country around Auch and Condom, in the heart of Gascony, home of the most famous of the musketeers, D'Artagnon. This is also goose land, but the most famous delicacies are small birds roasted on skewers, wrapped in vine leaves and popped in the oven, or put in paper boxes and roasted on a wood fire. The birds are ortolans or *becfigues*, but other game birds are popular, particularly when finally blazed with Armagnac or when the pungent brandy is used to finish the sauce. The country is also famous for *confits*, potted bits of fowl, game, or pork, and some of the oldest dishes of France, like *la galimafrée*, which is a ham stewed with vegetables; *la gasconnade*, which is pieces of mutton from the leg larded with anchovies and garlic, roasted on skewers over charcoal; *l'estouffat*, rump steak braised long in a rich stock strengthened with red wine and Armagnac; *la garbure*, a thick soup or thin stew—what the New Englanders call "victuals and drink"—full of vegetables, and often with pork, *confits*, bacon, and drippings, the solids served on slices of bread. There are many egg dishes, those *à la Vic* being baked on a dice of ham and served with tiny sausages called Vic *saucissons; à la Gasconne* are eggs fried on slices of eggplant, ham, and mashed tomatoes; *omelette landaise* is filled with slices of ham and baked on bread fried in goose drippings with onions.

The Mediterranean coast from Spain to Italy abounds in vineyards, mostly sweet wines in Corbières and Roussillon, good reds in Montpellier and rough ones from the Midi, the last of which are sold by the percentage of alcohol they contain. There are the districts of Tavel and Châteauneuf-du-Pape, near Avignon, which are classed as Rhônes. But the most interesting ones to visit are the Provence districts along the Riviera: Bandol, Bellet, La Palette, and Cassis, near Marseille. Not that the wine is best, for it's hard to choose between one and the other, but because the towns are so pretty, tucked under a pile of hills, the buildings curving around the crescent of the harbor, the cafés being a fine place to sit and watch the fishing boats, sipping the chill pink wine from the vineyards up behind, ordering a fish for lunch, then taking a long nap or a longer walk before a swim. In June and September the Riviera's not so crowded, but maybe that's part of the fun. And the wines taste like the best in the world with the local food.

Up the Rhône are the districts of Hermitage, Condrieu, and Château Grillet, and east of these are various small vineyards in the Savoie. East of Lyon is Bresse, whose chickens are also rated by *cru*, or region, as to where they come from. There are fish and crayfish from the mountain streams, mushroom and truffles, cream and butter. All of these get to Lyon, which is the gastronomic capital of France, not just because of the produce that flows in from the east, or the Charollais beef that is the best in France and comes from farms all around the city, but because just above is Burgundy.

Southern Burgundy produces the lesser wines but the best scenery, and the most popular wine in all the world —Beaujolais. The vineyards begin a scant twenty miles northwest of Lyon, and there's a saying that three rivers bathe the city, the Rhône, the Saône, and Beaujolais. This favorite French wine tastes best when it's drunk young, preferably the spring after the vintage and straight from the cask; its fresh and fruity taste is just right with the Bresse chicken, the fish dumplings from Nantua, and the Charollais beef. Wines simply labeled "Beaujolais" come from any place in the district, but the best of them bear the names of the townships, or communes, from which they come: Brouilly and Côte de Brouilly, Morgon and Fleurie, Moulin à Vent, and Chiroubles, Chénas, St.-Amour and Juliénas.

The main town of southern Burgundy is Mâcon, just above Beaujolais, and west of it is the district called the Maconnais, which produces the white peer of Beaujolais, Pouilly-Fuissé. The country is noted for *charcuterie*, especially a hot sausage stuffed with pistachio and truffle, just the food for picnics in the rolling landscape. Still further north is the Chalonnais, whose wines of Mercurey and Givry, Rully and Montagny, are often skipped over because of the fame of Beaujolais and the magnificence of the vintages from the heart of Burgundy lying just to the north, the Côte d'Or.

If the Golden Slope weren't the richest land in France it would be the poorest, goes the saying. It is certainly no scenic wonderland, just a slope about thirty miles long rising to form the western rim of the Burgundian plain. The main highway from Paris to the Riviera cuts through its lower tip, passing between the Montrachet vineyards, which produce the world's greatest dry white wine.

The wines from the various townships are so good that the best of them go to market bearing the names of the particular vineyards from which they come. The lightest and softest come from the southern half of the Golden Slope, called the Côte de Beaune, which takes its name from its main town, and the fullest and richest come from the northern half, called the Côte de Nuits, after its chief town, Nuits-St.-Georges.

The Beaune slope produces all the famous whites— Montrachets from the communes of Chassagne and Puligny; Corton Charlemagne from Aloxe-Corton; Meursault, Beaune, and a host of lesser ones of Santenay, Savigny, Beaune, Monthelie, and Auxey-Duresses—and such famous reds as Volnay, Pommard, Beaune, and Corton. The villages are pleasant to wander through, but Beaune is the main attraction, with its famous Hospice, in the courtyard of which is held the famous wine auction that attracts buyers from all over the world. The institution is supported by the proceeds from the auction, held each year on the second Sunday in November, the wines coming from the various vineyards donated to the institution. The lots of wine are called *cuvées*, which means vats, and are sold under the name of the donor, not the vineyard.

The big, full wines from the Côte de Nuits come from towns that have tacked the names of their greatest vineyards onto their own, a practice begun in the last century to sell the lesser township wines with famous names. That's why the best wines always contain a vineyard name in addition to the town names. Wines called simply Nuits-St.-Georges or Vosne-Romanée, Flagey-Échézeaux or Chambolle-Musigny, Morey-St.-Denis or Gevrey-Chambertin, can come from anywhere in the township named, and are a blend of lesser wines. The exceptions are the town of Fixin and those of Clos de Vougeot, the first because its excellent vineyards were not as famous as its neighbors, and the second because all its vines, except a small parcel producing a little white wine, are enclosed inside a great wall. Several townships produce small quantities of white wines, notably Nuits-St.-Georges, Chambolle-Musigny, and Clos de Vougeot. The Clos is the largest vineyard in Burgundy—125 acres—and has over fifty owners. The massive château in the vineyard is the scene of many banquets held by the Burgundian promotion organization called Les Chevaliers de Tastevin, whose slogan is, "Never in vain, always in wine." Wine from the Clos is so revered that it's a tradition for French troops to salute whenever they pass by.

Off to the north, by itself, is the district of Chablis, which produces the dry white wine traditionally served with oysters. It's the first stop for buyers heading for Burgundy from Paris, not just because the wine is so good, but because the local restaurant specializes in dishes cooked in Chablis, including trout, ham, and a dessert soufflé made in an orange.

The traditional capital of the ancient realm of Burgundy is Dijon, once famous for its wines, and now noted for its annual gastronomic fair, its fine restaurants, and two foods that ruin the taste of wine because they are so sharp: mustard and gingerbread. It also produces a currant syrup, cassis. You add a jigger to chilled white Burgundy to make *rince cochon*, rinsed pig, good for hangovers. This is the town where most people stay before spending a day touring the vineyards and cellars of Burgundy.

To the north is the Champagne district, whose capital is Reims, tunneled by vast cellars. The vineyards are to the south, around the Montagne de Reims and the wine towns of Ay and Épernay, as well as along a slope called the Côte de Blancs. The White Slope produces Champagnes from white grapes, the others producing Champagne from black grapes, pressed quickly so that no color is picked up from the skins. The countryside is full of small inns where you can find Champagne Nature, wine of the country that is not sparkling, but excellent. It's the bubbles that matter most, though, and all the firms are delighted at the chance to tell you how they got there.

Straight east is Alsace, with its capital of Strasbourg and its wine towns of Kaysersberg and Kientzheim, Riquewihr and Hunawihr, Ammerschwihr and Mittelwihr, Ribeauvillé, Bergheim, and dozens of others. The best wines come from what's called the Haut-Rhin, a vineyard section between the towns of Colmar and Sélestat. The district was ravaged during the war, but what was left, and even the rebuilt areas, is beautiful. Many a wine buyer dreams of finding the time to spend a summer in Alsace, someday.

The towns seem to be still in the Middle Ages, particularly Riquewihr, encircled by a wall. Stone arches of the walls and alleys are crowned with flower boxes, which are also hung in front of the windows of the low, stone houses. Vines hang above doorways, fruit trees are trained against walls, above the town are the foothills of the Vosges, below is the valley of the Rhine, and surrounding it are the green vineyards. In Kaysersberg, a stream runs right down the main street. It's a lovely place to be.

Well, you can't go everywhere. But you must go to the valley of the Loire, and it would be a crime not to have lunch in St.-Émilion, to sit by the harbor in Cassis. You could pass up the fabulous restaurants around Lyon and in the mountains of Savoie, picnicking in Beaujolais or Pouilly-Fuissé, wandering around the streets of Volnay and Pommard, the courtyard of the Hospice in Beaune, the great presshouse in Clos de Vougeot. The cellars of Ay, Épernay, and Reims aren't a must, unless you like Champagne. It's hard to imagine, though, how anybody could bring himself to miss Alsace. There's also the tasting to be done in Cognac and Armagnac. There's Calvados in Normandy—what a sight when the apple trees are in blossom, particularly in the Vallée d'Auge, which produces the best cider.

Every nook and cranny of France south of Paris has its vineyards, it seems, with delicious local wines that can't be shipped, and where there aren't wines there are liqueurs and cordials to be tasted. Each wine district produces its own *marc,* a distillation from the pulp left after the pressing. They are potent and leathery in taste, but magnificent after dinner, with coffee. And there are the distillates from fruits in Alsace: *fraise* from strawberries, *framboise* from raspberries, *quetsch* and *mirabelle* from plums. It's as hard to know where to stop as it is to know where to begin. You can be sure of one thing. You can't go far wrong in France, not in matters of eating and drinking.

BELGIUM

GASTRONOMY. Traders since ancient times, the Belgians have adopted food and drink from everywhere; court dishes from the ancient monarchies, repertoires from French, German, and Scandinavian cuisine, restaurant menus from Swiss hotel cooking, snack foods from Britain and America. Coffee and spices from the East, beer from Germany, wines from France and Iberia, tea from England, chocolate from the Dutch, soft drinks from America, have all been adopted. Fish from the coast, farm produce, and wildfowl and small game are common.

BREAKFAST. Coffee with hot milk, sometimes tea or chocolate. Bread and rolls, sometimes breakfast pastry, served with jams and jellies, and butter. Hotels serve Continental breakfast, but the English breakfast with tea and a coddled or boiled egg and possibly smoked fish, ham, bacon, or sausage, and the American breakfast, including fruits and various egg dishes, are available.

LUNCH & DINNER. Generally, a three- or four-course meal, with beer or wines, is normal. Lunch may be a simple soup or fish course followed by a meat or fowl course, dinner is apt to include both. Great variety of restaurants.

STREET FOOD.   Vast, including waffle and sausage stands, fried-potato and fish barrows, soup and shellfish carts, and many delicatessen counters, snack bars, pastry and teashops, ice-cream and milk bars.

The Belgians are pleased to have you know that they drink more beer than anybody else, naturally inclined that way because they have the strongest digestions in the world. "Lively as the competition is with other drinks, the Belgian remains faithful to his beer," goes one hand-out, pointing out that 250 pints per maw are downed each year, that there are 540 breweries in this country of 12,000 square miles and nine million people, at least a quarter of whom are children and ancients who shouldn't be drinking beer at all.

Any Belgian will tell you that French fries were invented in Belgium, probably in Brussels, and when you tell him that's enough to condemn any nation through eternity, he'll just laugh and say you haven't had *frites* in Brussels, yet, and that the Belgians also invented meat balls. He'll nod in agreement when you say Belgian food is reputed to be the best in the world, and proceed to give you details of *carbonnades*, those stews made with beer, and of *hochepots* containing all sorts of odd animal parts that sound quite inedible; then he'll wind up with several minutes about eels, the favorite Belgian food, describing cold pickled eel from Namur served *à l'escavèche*, or jellied, green eels served with herbs and vinegar, and the best of all, *friture* of baby eel, a pile of fried eels that almost wriggle on the plate. After you've bravely tried some of these, finding them almost delicate, and very good with beer, he'll send you off to a restaurant in Brussels, Au Trône Saint-Arnould, where everything is made with beer, even the ice cream. That's good, too.

Busily running himself down in the current European fashion, the Belgian will omit mentioning that his country imports more Burgundy than any other, as well as enormous quantities of Bordeaux, Champagne, white wines from Luxembourg and the Rhine, Sherry and Port, preferring to point out that the influence of the tourist has caused many restaurants to internationalize their menus and that they are becoming too French. Failing to mention that Belgian restaurants have an old tradition of preserving the ancient dishes, and of preparing the many specialties in the customary way, he will sigh lugubriously and say that the trouble with Belgians is that they eat too much, and are too easily satisfied. Then he'll ask if you don't think he's getting a little fat.

If you ask him about the specialties directly, he'll say yes, they're still around, but the Belgians prefer to eat foreign foods, and offer to give you his private list of excellent places in town to get Italian or Chinese or Spanish or Hungarian food. When you ask him point-blank if Belgian restaurants are really the best in the world, he'll say they are still good, but the best Belgian cooking is in the home, and that the trouble with the restaurants is that the Belgians have forgotten how to complain. He'll then tell you where you can get a really good English plum pudding, or a splendid American hot dog. But good food, simply cooked, is Belgium's glory.

Belgians love to eat, at home or out, and they have

great interest in and respect for national dishes and specialties of other countries, which they prepare with as much care and attention as they lavish on their own.

In addition to the beer heaven already mentioned, the following would probably appear on any Belgian's list of top Brussels restaurants: l'Ancienne Barrière, Le Thermidor, Le Cygne, Le Carlton, La Courronne, l'Epaule de Mouton, which is said to be run by a fantasist who invents things, Comme Chez Soi, which is said to be run by a maniac, Vincent's, which is noted for sea food, and Fond Roy, which is expensive, like all the others, but which serves probably the best lobster in town. Others include Villa Lorraine, Le Bonne Vieux Temps, La Rotisserie Ardennaise, and Le Prince d'Orange on the outskirts of town. There are dozens of others around Belgium, particularly in the Ardennes.

After wangling such a list from a local who eats out a lot because he entertains on an expense account, you are sure to be told that the best food in town is in the private clubs. When you ask how one gets into the private clubs, you are told that someone who's a member has to take you, and it's easy because just about everybody is a member. But tourists have no trouble on their own.

The private clubs exist, not because of snobbery but because of the drinking laws. There are restrictions on drinking hard liquor, evidently to keep up beer consumption, so the center of town is filled with moderate-sized, not-too-expensive, extremely handsome clubrooms that pride themselves on serving the best and freshest in the markets. Service is good, too.

Most of them are decked out in the old Flemish style, with comfortable chairs, beamed ceilings, paneled walls, paintings, tapestries, tail-coat captains and darting bus-boys. A few serve only light lunches, some are in the big hotels, and some are private rooms in public restau-rants. A list of good ones would include the very expen-sive Carlton, the Savoy, Le Cygne, Le Renard, Au Bon Vieux Temps, Dikenek's, the Brussels, the New Yorker, and the American Club.

But all these are special places, and a French gastronome might say the cooking is not as refined as that in Paris, which is a comment the Belgians often make. "Brussels is above all a capable housewife," says Gyory in the text for one of his travel books, and by that he doesn't mean that the city is full of women rushing home to cook things privately.

The very streets are full of places to eat, from the barrows selling perfectly browned chips, bought by the bag and dunked in a dollop of mayonnaise between bites, the carts of snails and oysters, the street-side stands serv-ing *gauffres de Liège*, sweet waffles fat and hot. Shops that are mostly counter sell cheese and sausage. The snack bars are full of all sorts of delicatessen: Ardennes ham smoked with juniper, barbecued chickens, soups. Fruit shops smell of orchards and always of the dark blue bunches of grapes from the vast hothouses just outside town. The side streets are full of small restaurants, where you can get all the specialties, and nobody should leave Brussels without trying every one.

Chicorée de Bruxelles, which Americans insist on call-ing endive, is served every which way, always with some sugar to remove any bitterness, and particularly stuffed with ground meat, or with ham and a white cheese sauce, or breaded and then browned lightly in the oven with a slice of ham and more cheese sauce. *Choux de Bruxelles* is never boiled until rank in Brussels, and if sprouts haven't been ruined for you forever by bad cooks, here's the place to learn to love the little Brussels cabbages.

Chœsels au madère is a stew of oxtail and other meats simmered and then cleared, then simmered covered in beer, after which tiny meat balls and plenty of mushrooms are added, the sauce being finally smoothed with Madeira until it glistens, or "blinks," to use the Brussels word.

Ballekes or *fricadelles* are the original Brussels meat balls, usually pork and veal but often ground leftovers, mixed with soaked bread crumbs, bound with egg and spiced with nutmeg, then braised in butter. They are often cooked with beer and in various stocks, and they are generally served with braised endive and mashed potatoes, along with a gravy boat full of hot brown sauce. They've become a specialty all over Scandinavia.

Le complet Bruxellois, or *moules et frites*, is just mussels steamed with a dice of celery and onions and finished with chopped parsley moistened in the pan juices, but it is served with the incomparable crisp *frites*, and it is one of the world's great dishes.

You can also get *Waterzoï*, a fricasee of chicken that originated in Ghent, the special broth for which is also used for veal, fish, and rabbit. The famous asparagus from Malines is on every menu in season, best when served with a parsley-and-butter sauce in which you mash an egg yolk. There's sure to be *carbonnade flamande*, the national stew of Flanders, made from beef collar, called spiring.

You don't have to venture into Flanders for jugged

hare or red cabbage with apples and breast of beef (*fleed*),
to Antwerp for green eels, to Liège for veal kidneys or
crayfish, to Brabant for blood sausages with potatoes and
apples called *boudins entre ciel et terre*, or to Ghent for
the original *hochepot*, which is a winter stew of all sorts
of meats and root vegetables, with pork sausages and
mealy potatoes, served as a soup and a main course. All
these are readily available in Brussels. The hop sprouts
from Alost, *les jets de houblon*, are available in the vegetable stalls for a few weeks beginning in March; they are
served with a *sauce mousseline* and poached or hard-
boiled eggs, or in a ham, tongue, and sausage salad with
mayonnaise, tomatoes, water cress and hard-boiled eggs.
And following along in their season are Wépion strawberries, St.-Trond cherries, and cheeses from Huy, Herve,
Knokke, Oray, Chimay, Namur and Liège.

But you ought to go to the country for the meat loaf
of Virton, *pâté de viande de Virton;* the goose of Vise,
l'oie a l'Instar; the Namur goose paste, *pâté d'oie Namu-
roise;* and to Ghent and Bruges for pastries, particularly
the *moques de Gand* and the *Nœuds de Bruges*.

Brussels has its own molded spice bread, like gingerbread, called *spéculos* or *spéculaus*, meant for St. Nicolas
feasts but obtainable all year round to accommodate
tourists and impatient Belgian youngsters. Similar to these
are the spice cookies called *couques de Dinant*, formed
into horseheads, lions, and grotesques. There are the long,
flat tongues of spice bread miscalled *pain à la Grecque*
and originally from Gracht. There are *cramiques* and
craquelines, the first a sweet bread with raisins, the second
a sort of sugary brioche. There's tough country bread,
baked over wood fires, sensibly called *pain de campagne*.

And there are thousands of others, for the Belgian is as mad about baked goods as he is about beer.

Oh yes. Back to the beer. There are *brasseries* all over the country where you can go for a beer or a cup of coffee or a snack, and where you can sit for hours, reading the paper or a book. They remind one of the Viennese coffeehouses, particularly those in Brussels, which is very reminiscent of Vienna, maybe just because of the *brasseries*.

Here you can get all the regular light beers, patterned after Pilsener and the German lagers. But you can also get special strong beers, those common in Brussels being *faro* and *lambic;* the best of these is Orval Trappiste, made by the monks. Then there are the aged beers from Roulers and Courtrai. There are seasonal beers from the Walloon country, and there's something called *krieke*, which is a beer with cherries that's sweet and sour, not necessarily just the thing for spare ribs. They're in the *brasseries*, just waiting to be tried.

There are a couple of local liqueurs, elixir de Spa and elixir d'Anvers, which ought to be tasted, and there's genièvre de Hasselt, a gin patterned after the spicy Dutch product. And there are the usual gamut of soft drinks, one worse than another, consumed eagerly by the younger set as they watch the color movies of bands and singers on the fancy juke boxes, rising every once in a while to twist or jitter between the snack-bar booths. As you see, there's something for everybody in Belgium, an endless variety, for every taste.

THE NETHERLANDS

GASTRONOMY. The Dutch cultivate their kitchen gardens and serve the produce with the riches of the sea, adding ham and cheese and the glories of Southeast Asia for variety, along with beer and gin, coffee and cocoa, to wash it down. Roasts and stews are popular in winter, cabbages and root vegetables being served with them, and year-round favorites are pancakes of various sizes, slathered with ginger and other jams. Wines are popular, not only French and German table wines, but the fuller Sherries and Ports.

BREAKFAST. Dutch oatmeal is just about the best in the world, but breakfast is usually bread and butter, with slices of ham and cheese, with coffee and milk. Tea, a coddled egg, and other parts of English and American breakfasts are available in most hotels.

LUNCH & DINNER. Lunch can be a hot dish, but is often bread, ham, and cheese, often served with a fried or coddled egg. Early dinner may be more of the same, but generally includes a stew, a roast, or some other hot dish, perhaps fish or fowl, in cold weather. Indonesian food is eaten in restaurants.

STREET FOOD. In the spring, barrows serve green herring, eaten with a squirt of lemon; pancakes and pastry are available in the bakeshops and teashops for midmorning and afternoon snacks. Cafés and snack bars serve delicatessen and sandwiches.

The Dutch eat warm in winter and cold in summer, and though they'd never say so you can tell they wonder why everybody else doesn't do the same. This delusion stems from the indubitable fact that spring begins in March and summer ends in September, according to the calendar, marking the cold-food season. But this doesn't take into account Dutch weather, glorious in spring, cool in summer, wet and cold the rest of the time, so the way of eating is simply a device to convince themselves that they really do have a summer, like everybody else. The clouds can pile a mile high, the nights can drop to fifty, the mornings can be gray and drizzly, but its summer, say the Dutch, the time for eating cold. And if the sun comes out, however weakly, they say, "See?"

The Dutch refuse to have anything to do with the idea that it's quantity and calories, not the temperature of the food, that makes you hot, which is why they serve the best breakfasts on the Continent. In addition to fine-textured white bread and rolls, and little pots of butter with petals spooned on top that make them look like yellow roses, there's also a coddled egg, a plate full of thinly sliced ham and thin, thin slices of cheese. The Dutch, like the Swiss, eat enormous quantities of cheese, at least partly out of patriotism, to keep up home consumption. Hot drinks go with breakfast: coffee, tea, or Dutch cocoa, although cocoa's a winter drink and the tea's a sop to the English tourist, who loves Holland, maybe because the weather's so similar.

After breakfast, everybody puffs off to work, most of them on bicycles. If there's a breathless air about the Dutch, it's because so many people are always panting slightly because of the pedaling. Certainly, passion does not flame in Amsterdam, but that's mostly because of the steep stairs. Land is so precious that little space is wasted on stairways; they are the steepest anywhere, and climbing them is like scaling ladders.

Ten o'clock is coffeetime, with cakes and biscuits. Sometimes there's *poffertjes,* pronounced "poffertish," more or less, and who can resist anything with a name like that? They're small, fat, buttery pancakes. A lunch of *koffietafel* lasts from noon through two, and lots of people pedal home on their breathless bikes. Teatime comes at three o'clock—more cakes and biscuits—and finally there's dinner from five to seven, which is more *koffietafel,* or maybe just *boterhammen,* which is slices of buttered bread with ham or cheese or something piled on. All of it cold, of course, except the tea, coffee, or chocolate.

"Don't you want just a plain normal cold lunch?" a Dutchman said to me, firmly, and when I quickly agreed, we went to the best place for *koffietafel* in town, Het Brouwerswapen, on Rembrandt Place, which for no bad reason boasts a park whose trees are strung with colored lights that are lit even in daylight—sometimes.

"How would you like your egg?" said the waiter, and I said fried, and asked for beer, which surprised him. He returned with three platters: the bread platter contained white bread, dark rye, French bread, rusks not as hard as the Holland rusks we know, raisin bread, crackers, and two kinds of soft roll, a twist and a sort of hot-dog bun. The meat platter contained slices of ham, roast beef, veal, frankfurter, a pâté, lettuce, tomato wedges, and small piles of sweet and sour pickles. The cheese tray contained thin slices of Edam and caraway. He also brought marmalade and raspberry jam in little pots, some butter and pots of coffee. Just like breakfast, you see, only more so, and when I'd asked about the beer, and he'd told me you don't usually have beer at *koffietafel,* the waiter whisked away our plates and returned with a platter of fruit: apples, oranges, bananas, and a small basket of cherries. When we'd eaten all the cherries, and pocketed bananas for later, he said, "And how about some pastry?" We declined. The place was full of cheery Dutchmen, all breaking custom and eating warm—bowls of soup, fish, veal, and chicken dishes. Presumably, they hadn't been told it was the time to eat cold, or else they were protesting against the weather.

I asked about this later, and was told they were all probably entertaining foreigners, and they'd certainly eat cold that night. Even the local men's group that was having steaks and beer? That's different, it must have been some sort of celebration.

The dinner hour, at least, is not honored in the breach, for everybody seems to be through by seven, except the tourists and those Dutch entertaining foreigners. Entertaining foreigners is, of course, an almost daily task, and while the ancient custom of eating cold is certainly honored every day during the summer, if only at breakfast, morning coffee, teatime, and late at night, the Dutch temper their tradition with tolerance, eating warm whenever called upon, to be sociable.

They have good reason to. Among other things, Dutch veal is the best in the world. The reason for this, say the Dutch, is that they don't have room to let the calves grow up. This is also the Swiss argument, the Welsh argument, the Belgian argument, and the Scandinavian argument. One needn't take it too seriously. Dutch veal is very, very good, as it is everywhere in non-Mediterranean Europe. The seasonal fare comes promptly to city tables to make such luncheon dishes as asparagus with melted butter, sprinkled with nutmeg and served with a boiled egg, and young beans called *tuinbonen*, served with ham from Gelderland, and plover's eggs in April. Garden vegetables like tomatoes, peas and lettuce, fruits like strawberries and cherries get an early start in the brilliant spring, ripening slowly in the cool moist summer.

The cold-weather hot dishes, *winterkost*, include cabbage with wurst, *boerenkool;* cabbage with ham, *zuurkool;* white cabbage with pork chops and boiled potatoes; and red cabbage with apples. There's *hachée*, onions and chopped beef braised together, and served with potatoes, there's *hete bliksem*, which is an apple-and-potato dish. And when the weather is in between, the cold lunch may begin with one of the many soups, the most famous of which is probably pea soup, *ertensoep*, or with an omelet, or a hot vegetable with a sauce, or the "bouncer," *uitsmijter*, which is ham and eggs. Such a meal might end with a special dessert, the most typical of which is hard to find today. That's *watergruwel*, a pudding made out of a sort of red currant. Or lunch might be a thin, hot pancake more than a foot across, slathered with ginger jam or raspberry or strawberry preserves, or simply buttered and sprinkled with sugar.

Good plain food, one might conclude, but that's ignoring the adventurous past of the Dutch and their long familarity with Africa, the Caribbean, Indonesia, and China. Trade in spices drew Dutch merchantmen all over the world, not only for nutmeg and ginger, cocoa and Cayenne, cinnamon and pepper, vanilla and allspice, but also such warming drinks as tea and coffee, rum, Curaçao and Batavia Arrack, French wines, Sherries and Port. Dutch sailors taught English tars how to make mulled port with cinnamon, which came to be called "bishop," the famous hot punch of post-Elizabethan England. And a Dutchman invented gin, a peppery infusion of juniper berries that warmed the cold cockles of the poor for generations.

Orient treasures of exotic dishes were brought to Europe by the Dutch. There's *sateh*, skewers of broiled meat; *bahmi*, a noodle dish; *loempiahs*, stuffed Chinese pancakes. Curries, *nassi goreng*, fried rice with side dishes, and the *rijsttafel*, are as much a part of Netherlands cuisine as cabbage or cheese. Restaurants like the Bali and the Azie, Fong Lie and Waroeng Djarva, Taiton and China, offer some of the best Far Eastern cookery in Europe, and the Lido is said to offer the finest *rijsttafel* anywhere. The "rice table" is many dishes of spicy sauces, the most illustrious being a chili sauce called *sambal oelek*, and titbits eaten with rice. Nobody with any curiosity at all would leave Holland without trying several versions. As for curries, it's wise to remember that the yellow curries are the mildest, the green are the hottest, and a glass of beer should be close by for oral cooling.

The most fascinating restaurants are those denominated *Oudhollands,* decorated in Old Dutch style and serving specialties and international dishes with Dutch flair. The narrowest of these is De Groene Lanteerne, which is only a doorway wide at the entrance, scarcely a dozen feet from side to side once you're in. The Green Lantern has an upper deck which seems to be just the place to eat *schuttersmaaltijd,* which is a sort of casserole of steak, chicken, and ham, in a veal sauce with mushrooms, served with peas and fried potatoes. All the other Old Dutch restaurants—Binnenhofje, Flessig, 't Swarte Schaep, Hollands Glorie, 't Gekroont Spinnewiel, and the rest—serve this dish and other famous "warms." But perhaps the favorite of visitors to Amsterdam is D. Vijff Vlieghen, a restaurant called the Five Flies, whose version is called "Moeder Hendrien," after one of the early cooks.

The Five Flies is one of the best examples of the modern European philosophy—it's more than just a policy—of running an eating place. It is contained in five connecting houses that have been restored to make an atmosphere of the Amsterdam townhouse of several centuries ago, with old paneling and tiles and objects from past days. Each house is a separate room with its own character, and a party of a dozen or more can reserve one of the rooms for privacy. Upstairs, there's a Bride's Room, where a honeymoon couple can dine by themselves, listening to the sentimental tunes from an old music box, if they wish, at a price so low that you have to reserve the space well before the honeymoon. The upstairs of the original house is the bar, presided over by Wim, a bartender who performs sleight-of-hand between mixing drinks. He acts as a sort of message center for the international clientele whose first stop in Amsterdam is always the Five Flies, and he is occasionally inveigled into flying to England and elsewhere for a week end to provide the merriment for a special fancy "do." The chef is considered the best in Holland, a white-haired encyclopedia of Dutch specialties who is always being hustled off to fairs and outlying embassies to put on special demonstrations or prepare banquets. The waiters are experts, without servility, interested in giving guests what would taste best to them at the moment, and able to make apt suggestions about the menu and the wine list. There's a weekly meeting of the whole staff, to figure out ways to make things still better. "You can have good food everywhere," says the manager, "but you can eat in the Five Flies only in Amsterdam." There's a special businessman's lunch each day, because the restaurant wants to appeal to local residents as well as travelers, and prices are reasonable.

One of the Dutch specialties is a veal steak with cherries, and another is *palingsoep*, a rich and delicate bisque that includes smoked eel. Even the herring is served a special way, on a bed of crushed ice in wooden bowls carved in the shape of fish, with diced onions and slices of tomato. They make a point of suggesting a typical Dutch drink as an apéritif, Roode Bessen, a chilled glass of red currant Genever made by Lucas Bols. The favorite dessert is Fantaisie, an ice cream adored by children because it's served with sparklers and candy wafers decorated with a picture of the original building, which was once owned by a man named Flieghen.

The Dutch devour green herring in the spring, tiny fish picked up off the street carts by the tail and mouthed in a single bite. Later, when they're too big for that, the herrings are placed on beds of ice and served as a first course.

In addition to the restaurants, there are the snack bars, *broodjeswinkels,* where good, cheap meals can be had in a hurry. Popular ones are Broodje van Kootje, Van Dobben, Frits de Ruijter, the Hot Dog, and the various Ruteck's restaurants and cafeterias, which are a chain with branches all over Holland. The famous Dutch breweries Heineken's and Amstel, run restaurants, and those in the hotels are exceptional. The Hotel de Poort van Cleve has over a hundred ways of preparing beef, and during the winter they feature pancakes some of which are twenty inches across; fathers visiting their offspring in the universities invariably bring them here for dinner, to recapture old memories. Two favorite meeting places are the American Hotel and the Krasnapolsky, the first with its terraces and cafés on the Leidseplein, the second with its enormous restaurants on the Dam, opposite the royal palace; the food is varied, good, plentiful, and reasonable in both places. Prices are higher in the big international hotels like the Europe, the Amstel, and the Hilton.

Each year, the tourist office issues a little folder listing various restaurants by category, including not only the Old Dutch ones, but also inexpensive ones, tearooms or buffets, snack bars, and those featuring Indonesian, Chinese, French, Italian, Jewish, Swiss, and Danish food, not to mention fish restaurants, all complete with address and phone number. It is quite impartial, but any Dutch friend will tick off the ones that are best at the moment, adding a few suggestions of his own.

There are several wine houses where you can taste the various vintages with snacks, among them Marianne's and Ognibenni. Restaurants that feature cheese include Keff and the Fromagerie Crignon. The cordial-producing firms of Lucas Bols and Wynands Fockink run restaurants in conjunction with their establishments.

One word about the bakeshops: Cookies and chocolate with nuts in them seem to be particular Dutch favorites, and the cakes called *Rotterdammertjes* and *Amsterdammertjes* are not to be missed. From the street stands you ought to be able to get delicious *frits*, eaten in the hand while listening to one of the street organs that are a fixture. A favorite children's food is French fries and applesauce, the last a dessert that should not be missed in Holland. It's also the custom to wish someone well before eating in Holland, in fact it's impolite not to, and the most common phrase is *"Eet smakelijk"*—roughly *et smah-kuh-licht*. It means "eat well," and it's hard not to, anywhere in the Netherlands.

SCANDINAVIA

GASTRONOMY.   Smoked, fresh, or pickled, boiled, fried, or stewed, fish and sea food form the basis of the Scandinavian cuisine, astoundingly augmented by an infinite variety of open-faced sandwiches and delicatessen, called *Smørrebrød, koldt bord* or *smörgåsbord*, depending on what country you're in. Augmented by farm produce, veal, ham, and bacon, dairy and poultry products, the cuisine takes on variety, and in the north these are extended with hams made from lamb, bear, and reindeer, mountain cheeses, trout and wildfowl, venison and a variety of stews. Crisp flat breads, various forms of clotted milk and cream, superb baked goods, and glorious goose and duck dishes set the cuisine apart.

BREAKFAST.   All sorts of porridge and cold American cereals, but a common breakfast is bread, rolls or pastry, and coffee.

LUNCH.   A buffet, like the *koldt bord* or *smörgåsbord* is rarer than it used to be, but open-faced sandwiches, eaten with knife and fork, are the rule. Aquavit and beer are usually drunk with these, followed by pastry and coffee.

DINNER.   Generally early, before seven, and frequently including a soup and usually a fish, followed by a hot

stew or roast or grillade, with beer or wines. There
are lavish holiday spreads in all the restaurants at Christmas, and much hot punch.

STREET FOOD. Herring barrows in the spring, countless slot machines purveying sandwiches, fruit, and
candies, many sandwich shops, pastry shops, and bars
where dairy products and delicatessen are served, and
many cafés where tea, soft drinks, and beer are most
popular, but where sandwiches, tea, and pastry can be
had.

DENMARK

Scandinavia is a group of states bound together by the
sea and a sailing heritage that goes back beyond the longboats of Leif the Lucky. Denmark looks north to the
spine of mountains shared by Norway and Sweden, east
to the forests and lakes of Finland, west to the mammoth
islands of Iceland and Greenland. All of them look south
to Europe, west to America and east to Russia with a
fascinated neutral gaze, and with all their individual differences, what they have most in common today is fish,
probably herring. Marinated herring, spiced herring, rollmops, smoked herring, and herring in dozens of sauces,
become part of every Danish lunch or dinner.

  The Danes have let themselves be carried away by the
popularity of their open-faced sandwiches, *Smørrebrød*,
and some are not quite sure the degeneracy into ornate-
ness and overloading isn't the fault of excessive American
enthusiasm and possibly to active promotion. There are,
officially, at least a couple of hundred recognized vari-

eties; there's a weekly Danish Lunch where tourists are instructed in the art of making *Smørrebrød;* the Oskar Davidsen restaurant, which was for years the most famous open-face spot in Copenhagen, has a list over five feet long; Stephen A'Porta's is not much shorter, and most restaurants have a page or two, on which you tick off the ones you want, starting with herring or sardine open sandwiches, or the biggest treat of all, tiny Greenland shrimps. These are excellent with a cold glass of *snaps,* followed by one of the two Danish beers, Carlsberg or Tuborg. The aquavit is not sipped but gulped, swigged mouthfulls at a time, often chased with draughts of beer. Salmon, smoked or boiled, anchovies, mussels—or whatever fish is in season, boiled bits of sole, cod, even trout —are other choices.

This first *Smørrebrød* is followed by one of ham, liverwurst, or sausage; or perhaps one with a cold slice of beef, veal, pork, or chicken; or maybe one of tomato and egg, or peas and carrots, asparagus, or other vegetables, generally bound in mayonnaise, sharpened with bacon or anchovy, and often decorated with dices of jellied consommé.

For a third sandwich, cheese is usually the choice, but Danes often go on to a hot dish: those meat balls called *Frikadeller;* roast loin of pork cooked with the rind and served with red cabbage sprinkled with caraway, or garnished with apples or currant jelly; ham, broiled or sautéed; or perhaps braised beef rolls filled with ham or pork and chopped parsley, and called *Benløse Fugle,* boneless birds.

If the *Smørrebrød* doesn't appeal at the moment, there's always the *koldt bord,* which is arrangements on a plate, just like *Smørrebrød*, but without the buttered bread. A Danish meal usually starts with one or the other, and a glass of aquavit.

The best open sandwiches are ones that don't have too many things on them, no matter how decoratively they are arranged; the combinations should add to and bring out the flavors of the various ingredients. The simple change from white to dark bread changes the taste, and even governs the amounts of what's piled on top. Americans are usually surprised by the thick layer of butter slathered on, but the butter acts as a constant that carries through from one sandwich to another, regardless of what's above and below. Although they can be eaten with the fingers, the smeared breads are usually piled so high that a knife and fork is needed. The *Smørrebrød* is, of course, an extension of the Dutch *koffietafel*, where you make your own combinations from the platters of breads, meats, and cheeses, and which are also eaten with a fork. The Danes simply go a step further, to make room for all the fish.

There are sausage stands everywhere, as in Vienna. It's possible to spend days in Copenhagen without going to a real restaurant at all, eating in the *Smørrebrød* bars, the snack bars, the sidewalk cafés, and buying goodies from the bakeshops and the endless vending machines, which purvey everything from fruit to nuts.

Danish pastry is called Vienna bread in Denmark, for no good reason, and it's always light and melting, never heavy and doughy like the American imitations. The Hôtel d'Angelterre is famous for its baked goods, and its sidewalk café is a perfect place to try some. The best bakery is said to be Van Hauen's, but then, all Danish

bakeries are superb, being one of the glories of the country.

Denmark, like all the countries along the Atlantic coast,
is a favorite of English tourists, so the tea is excellent,
always made in a pot, and served with a pitcher of hot
water. It's fine with pastry, but Danish coffee is better.

Copenhagen isn't the city to avoid restaurants in,
though. It's not called wonderful Copenhagen for nothing. There's the Tivoli, with its boys' band in red uniforms and black busbies—a fine Danish comment on the
proper use of things military—the pantomime theater,
the week-end fireworks, the colored lights and strollers,
the dancing and gaming, and the twenty restaurants, best
of which is Belle Terrasse, whose cuisine is international,
closely followed by Divan I and Divan II, whose food
is mostly Danish. But there are the hot dog, hamburger,
beef, and sausage stands, the candy fluff (not as good as
American fluff, it is reported to me, being not so synthetic
in taste), the pastry and sandwich booths, the buffets,
the terraces, the cafés. Belle Terrasse is the place for
dinner, if you can get in and want to spend a long time,
but the two Divans are places if you want to eat and
dawdle a bit while waiting for the fireworks, and both are
good for lunch, when the Tivoli is almost peaceful. Every
city should have an amusement garden right in the center
of town. There are all the other parks, too, ringing the
old city, including the one with the most nonchalant
niteries in the world.

The Danes are particularly proud of the Terminus,
the hotel right near the central station beside the Tivoli
Gardens. Its cooking is international, but there are specialties on the menu, including *gravad laks*, salmon that's

buried in a sweetened brine with bunches of fresh dill, under weights, and tiny shrimp, mussels, and lobster. But the thing here is service in the old, courtly tradition, smiling, deft, and unobtrusive, and the room fairly sings with quiet good cheer.

Also proud of its *gravad laks* is Frascati's on the City Hall Square, the Radhuspladsen, the Tivoli Gardens. Some people think it's the best in town, and it's one of the handsomest, a great sidewalk café and a series of small, neat rooms, decorated in July with thousands of carnations that have been matured in Africa from Danish plants, then flown home to glorify Frascati's. There you can get Danish *Frikadeller*, the meat balls that differ from the Belgian originals in that they are thickened with flour and milk and bound with egg whites, or the yolks and cream, and seasoned only with grated onion, salt, and pepper before sautéeing. The idea is to add as much milk and stir as much as possible over a period of time, to make them light. They are traditionally served with creamed asparagus, well parsleyed. Other typical dishes are Danish baby lamb or the spring lamb from Greenland, served with first peas; or poached salmon, invariably served with spinach.

Just as pleased with their *gravad laks, Frikadeller*, and lamb are the restaurants in the various hotels: the d'Angelterre and the Imperial, the Hafnia and Richmond, the Royal and the Viking Room in the Palace, not to mention the Bellevue just out of town, and Kystens Perle, up along the coast south of Elsinore. The last is famous for its Swedish cuisine. On top of the Codan Hotel, near the waterfront, is a dining room with a fine view of the old town, and a famous cold buffet.

A favorite tourist place is 7 Smaa Hjem, because the seven rooms are decorated in various periods; the same management runs 7 Nations, a large restaurant that serves fine international food. Krog's, on the waterfront, is the most famous fish restaurant, but there's also Fiskehuset. Across the canal is Gilleleje, which is noted for steaks and chops; there's Karen Kik's in the Slotskaelderen, which is noted for good, plain, cheap, old-fashioned Smørrebrød; and for not too expensive restaurants there are Stadil's, Skandia, or Grønningen.

There are no restrictions on drinking in Denmark, except the high price on imports, so schnapps from the state-owned distillery in Aalborg provides the most popular drink. Aquavit is high-proof spirits flavored with cumin, and there are at least four kinds, one more cuminy than the next: Roed is the lightest, whitest, most popular and cheapest; Extra, made for export, is slightly fuller in cumin; Jubilaeum is yellow and average in cuminess; and Brøndum is green and loaded with cumin. All are worth several tries, especially Jubilaeum. The way to drink it is to catch a pretty girl's eye, then sip, gazing deeply all the time. You say skål before sipping, naturally, pronounced skohl.

There's not much choice about beer, there being only the two, both produced by foundations that have some sort of relationship, because even the Danes can't tell the difference. That called Export is stronger, so everybody orders it. There are special types called Viking, F.F., and Elephant, which are stronger than the standard pilsener type.

The great Danish liqueur is Cherry Heering, blended right in Copenhagen from cherries crunched in August at the main orchard in Dalby, where there are 20,000 trees. The firm gets the produce of another 150,000 trees from other parts of Denmark. They have, incidentally, been able to keep the birds from attacking the ripening fruit by using a recording of the scream of frightened starlings. It's pretty unnerving to the farmhands, too. The cherry liqueur is often served with desserts, even with cheeses, and it's good with fruits, even ripe cherries.

NORWAY

Oslo is practically across the water from Copenhagen, up at the end of a fjord, one of the hundreds along the Norwegian coast, all of which are full of fish. Frogmen go diving in the far north ones for clamshell scallops, the trawlers bring in tons of fish to Bergen from the North Atlantic, and there are salmon streams everywhere—the best salmon in the world, say the Norwegians. If you observe that the Gaspé is noted for its salmon, as is the Columbia, not to mention the Scottish streams, a Norwegian may say that anybody is entitled to his opinion, but cold waters produce the best fish. The Danes, for instance, get their salmon from the warmer island waters in Botnik Bay; their sole is best but not their salmon. And if you mention to your Norwegian that the Gulf Stream keeps Scandinavia temperate, he'll say it doesn't flow into the fiords.

The Norwegians are also wild about herring, but the winter favorite is cod, worth a special trip to Bergen, so you can taste it in its home port, straight from the liveliest fish market in the world. High above the town is the Fløyrestaurant on top of nearby Fløyen mountain, and in Old Bergen is the Elsesro. Every place serves *fiske-pudding*, a hot mousse of pounded cod bound with eggs and cream, spiced with nutmeg and served with a lobster sauce, Cardinal. This great dish is said to be better in Norway than anywhere else in Scandinavia, where cod and herring are treated with the respect they deserve, even though they are plentiful. Fish is never really boiled, for instance; you can't even say it's poached or simmered, being gently lowered into a water or stock bath that is scarcely beading, so that the fish is allowed to draw, or *trekker*, the heat from the steaming liquid.

Fish has its seasons, and the boiled cod ends in April, the last of the R months, and people eat coalfish, *sei*, pronounced tsigh-ee and often called rock salmon or green cod, while they wait for the sea trout, which comes in on the fifteenth of May. The mackerel also starts in May, preceded by the *steinbut*, or ocean catfish, but the sea trout is the great summer fish.

On Independence Day, May 17, everybody celebrates by having the first salmon, but this is really early, the main salmon season being June and July. The baby scallops and fiord shrimp, and the blueshells, or mussels, also arrive in May, continuing at their best through July.

September is the month for the mountain trout, and the cod is back by October. There are oysters, but they're too expensive, and every Thursday there is herring—thirty or forty different dishes may be offered on the *koldt bord*—and there's grilled halibut and all the other fish. The big event of summer comes in August, when the crayfish appear. Nobody thinks highly of lobster when crayfish is available, but eyes brighten when crab appears in the fall.

The Norwegian *koldt bord* is a way of having a large breakfast and a light lunch, or the other way around. The cold table is set up by seven and usually gone by ten, and in spite of the name includes a variety of hot dishes—eggs, ham and bacon, fish, a meat stew—but many Norwegians like to have a breakfast of rolls and coffee, perhaps starting with cold cereal in summer and hot porridge in the winter. Lunch can be a sandwich or a snack from a *koldt bord*, or perhaps a bowl of soup or a hamburger from one of the many snack bars, which have become the rage in Oslo, where they go by such names as Wimpy Ekspress and Vikings Kafeteria. A vegetable soup not to be missed is *småmat*, which contains chipped beef, with a dice of veal, beef, and potatoes. Then there's Restaurant Blom which serves *sorte gryte*, the black pot, an ancient Norwegian stew.

The best lunch of all is served on Thursdays at still another Frascati's, which overlooks the Student's Grove in front of the National Theater, standing at the head of the long park that runs beside Karl Johans Gate, the main shopping street of downtown Oslo. In the race for modernity, the owner of Frascati's noted that the old Norwegian specialties were disappearing. It was harder and harder to find the country sausages that used to be made in every town in Norway, not to mention those of mutton and reindeer. The smoked leg of lamb, *fenalår*, reared by the sea but aged and air-dried in the mountains, to be served with scrambled eggs, the bear hams and *spekeskinke*, air-cured hams, were also hard to get. Where was the saddle of reindeer, the venison, and what about *faar i kaul*, that glory of good cabbage and good mutton with peppercorns, not overboiled? Even *gammelost*, the brown

Viking cheese that used to be on every table and distinctive in every village, was getting hard to come by. The homemade beers, so good there was a competition every year at Skarogne on the coast to pick the best—these never got to Oslo. And *raumegraut*, that smooth and rich hot porridge served with a gob of butter and sprinkled with cinnamon and sugar, made from sour cream and coarse brown oat flour, always served on Midsummer Eve and during the haying season—that never appeared on menus any more.

The Saga Lunch was the result, a tremendous buffet that includes all the country specialties that can be found, served with beer, light or dark, and topped off with coffee and cloudberries, *multer*, which are served with cream and are meant to be crushed with the tongue, not chewed, because they are full of seeds. There's the firm and tender flesh of smoked mackerel, served hot or cold, and all kinds of herring, and some country pâtés. There's a hot fish casserole and an assortment of breads and the crackerlike flatbreads that go best with the pronounced, sharp and clean tastes. The Saga Lunch is a way to become familiar with many of the old Norwegian specialties at once, so that when touring the country you'll know what to look for.

Across the fiord, in Bygdøy, reached by a ferry from in front of the town hall, are the ship museums, including the Kon Tiki and the Viking longboats, and also the folk museum and park containing examples of old country houses. In one of these a dinner of country dishes is served each day, to the tunes of a country fiddler. The Saga Lunch is much more extensive, and both should not be crowded into one day.

The Norwegians, sticking to old custom, eat dinner a little after four o'clock, perhaps so the long summer evening or the long winter night will be free for frolic. They may have a sandwich at nine or ten, to tide them over to breakfast. The restaurants begin serving at four and most people have finished eating by seven, unless they are entertaining foreigners. Even so, dinner is early, and foreigners are most apt to be taken to the Frognerseteren, high above the city, where trout is the specialty, particularly fried trout in sour cream; to the Holmenkollen, near the famous ski jump and museum; to the Ekeberg near the Navigation Academy and overlooking the fiord and the city; or the Kongen or the Dronningen, the King and the Queen, on the water, and run by local boating clubs. If the time is autumn, you will be able to order elk steak, reindeer chops, or roast reindeer with lingonberries and sour-cream sauce. Wildfowl like ptarmigan (*fjellrype*) and duck, woodcock, or capercailzie are to be had. The hotels also have these specialties, and in addition to the Bristol and the Grand there are the Astoria, the Continental, and the K.N.A., run by the Royal Automobile Club. The Bristol is particularly noted for its Christmas table, a groaning board that every restaurant establishes in the weeks before Christmas, each trying to outdo the other in variety and splendor. This Scandinavian custom is hard on the waistline, but everybody thinks it's a fine way to celebrate the festive season.

A fine new restaurant in town is the Fregatten, down on the wharf near the East Railroad Station. It serves the best fish in town, and it's the place for steamed cod with drawn butter, for sea trout served with new potatoes and sliced cucumbers, for wintertime stockfish, *lutefisk*, which is still one of the great favorites around the Mediterranean, and for whatever else happens to be in season at the moment. The Norwegians insist that fat fish like cod, particularly those served with the liver and roe, taste best with red wines, and they'll encourage you to try a Pomerol or Beaune, although nobody is upset if you have a white Graves or Meursault, or one from the Rhine or Loire.

The best *gravad laks* in Scandinavia may come from the Fregatten, who also bury mackerel and herring in the strong brine of sugar and salt, with much dill. After two days, some brandy, some Sherry, and some hoppy wort from the local brewery is added, with a little more sugar, salt, and white pepper. There it rests under weights for ten days, after which it is thinly sliced and served with mustard sauce and dill potatoes, and white wine or beer. It is glorious.

The same group manages the Kon Tiki and the Gondolen, out in the new exhibition hall near the airport, which serves some of the best food in town. There's a large cafeteria attached to it, and a place to dance, following the modern European trend of having a group of restaurants of different sizes and prices together, so that you can eat lavishly or simply, knowing that all the food is well prepared.

Dancing is a problem for the Norwegians because they have to order food with drinks, and if they wish to spend an evening on the town, that means eating two dinners. Some, of course, pass up the regular four o'clock dinner, but a Norwegian isn't happy about doing so. Drinking is also a problem, because only wines are available on the week end. "There's no liquor on Saturday or Sunday because we export so much fish," a girl explained to me. "It's a way to keep up wine consumption." The Norwegians turn fish into wine by selling much of the former to France, Spain, and Italy, taking the latter in exchange and solving the consumption problem on week ends, when there's time to do it justice.

The difficulty ceases to exist during the winter, when most of the night spots opened for the tourist season close, so people stay at home on week ends, solving their national problem. Also, during the winter, they drink a lot of aquavit, to counteract the gloom. And they continue drinking beer, which is also a problem, particularly the Export, pale or dark, which is 7 per cent alcohol. Norway so likes its Export beer they drink 90 per cent of it, although occasionally turning to a light Pilsen type or to Bayer, which is sweet and malty. These last two are only 4.75 per cent alcohol.

SWEDEN

The Swedes persist in the same early dining hour as the Norwegians, invariably being well into their dinners by five o'clock. The only way to find out the real spirit of Scandinavia, to find out what the Swedish and Norwegians do during the long evening, is to follow suit. This involves getting involved with the locals, which will certainly involve aquavit, called *schnapps* or maybe *brännvin* in Swedish, and drunk cold in thimble-sized V-shaped stemmed glasses. The unspiced *Renat* and *Taffel* are the most popular for regular drinking, but each region has its own special spiced version, meant primarily for drinking by itself or after meals, although they are also served with sandwiches and *smörgåsbord*. There's *Overste* and

Fänkål and *Ödåkra,* which are lightly spiced, *Herrgårds,* which is darker and aged in Sherry casks, *Skåne,* which is from the south and made from potatoes and well flavored with caraway, and *Norrlands,* from the north and made from alcohol derived from pine trees. There's aquavit flavored with *Angostura* and called that, and aquavit flavored with black currants, called *Svarta vinbär.* Then there's Swedish *punsch,* the best of which is *Grönstedts Blå,* and the winter drink called *glögg,* which is hot spiced red wine with almonds and raisins. The most popular beer is really near beer, like our near beer, and comes in three flavors: Pilsner, Lager, and Royal, which is pale ale. Even so, the Swedish drink most of their own Export beer, which is called Three Crowns, and which is nearly 5 per cent alcohol by volume. They are also very fond of clarets, Sherries, and Ports. And yet the Swedish are not known to be particularly heavy drinkers, the many signs you see reading BAR in the streets of Stockholm indicating a cafeteria or self-service milk bar, which is where people go for lunch, and where they drink milk with their sandwiches. It's hard for a tourist to figure out just what they do with their time, because the night clubs close in winter, as in Norway.

Scandinavian women, and the many children, drink great quantities of soda pop, including *Sockerdricka* which is a sort of lemonade, *Frisco,* which also tastes of lemon, *Pommac* which tastes of fruit, *Grappo* which tastes of grapefruit, and *Solo* or *Loranga,* tasting of orange. There's an endless range of fruit juices, squashes called *saft,* and wine imitations without alcohol.

Toasting the women is a frequent Scandinavian practice, starting with the one on your right. You raise your glass, catch her eye, smile, nod, say "*skål,*" sip and smile again, all the time looking in her eyes, raise the glass, then put it down. The host and hostess toast around the table, but you are not supposed to toast them back, responding with a smile, a nod, or a murmured "*tack-tack*," which is the way to say, "Thank you," "O.K.," "Yes," and a variety of other things. One says it many times, all day.

Anyway, early dinner is delicious in Sweden, which is full of foreign restaurants, some of them enormous— Berns', for instance, which has an outdoor café with a band that must be heard to be believed, a café, a sort of opera house of a dining room with theater, and a Chinese Pavilion, to mention a few. Other similar vastnesses are Riche, Salonger, Cecil's, Djurgårdsbrunns Wärdshus, Trianon, and Bacchi Wapen. Unbelievable.

In the Old Town are restaurants with historical looks and modern menus like Restaurant La Ronde, Den Gyldene Freden, and Frati's Källare, which also runs Tre Remmare in the center of town. In the Hötorgcity, or new city, is Cajsa Warg, named after a famous eighteenth-century cook, featuring Swedish specialties.

The first sign of spring in Stockholm is when the restaurant verandas go up in April. They are not exactly sidewalk cafés, for they are often glassed and covered with awnings, and the most glamorous of these is the Operakällaren in the Opera House, where you can get the best *Kåldolmar* in Stockholm. This is stuffed cabbage roll, not to be confused with *Kålpudding*, which is cabbage and minced meat. *Köttbullar*, which is meat balls, served with mashed potatoes, lingonberries, and cucumbers, for which the Swedish are famed, are generally smaller than *Frikadeller*. They also have fine *får i kål*, the Swedish version of cabbage and mutton.

The Operakällaren is really a group of restaurants served from a central kitchen, there being a long and gracious formal dining room, several small dining rooms and banquet rooms, a restaurant for the staff and players of the opera house, and a snack bar which is the best bargain in town. The sous-chefs each take turns to provide a special dish each day. They are allowed a free hand to make what they want, and they try to outdo one another. It's the sort of restaurant that shouldn't be mentioned, because now it will be mobbed by tourists. It's always crowded, anyway.

Across the water from the Operakällaren is the Grand Hotel, the most splendid in town, and moored before it is a three-masted schooner turned into a youth hostel, which is managed by a lady who was the head mistress of the Ethiopian emperor's Boys' School. It serves a marvelous buffet, and is harder to get into than the Grand Hotel. Other hotels, and restaurants like Teatergrillen, Ostermalmskällaren, Wardshuset Stallmästaregården, and the suburban Värdshuset Postiljonen, also serve exceptional international dishes and such Swedish specialties as *plättar*, which are tiny pancakes with lingonberries; a parfait made from cloudberries, which are called *hjortron* in Swedish; and perhaps even Sailor's Beef, a dish made from the tenderloin. Perch or salmon is simmered in a court bouillon with dill and served with dill and a special white sauce enriched with chopped hard-boiled eggs and dill.

A dish it would be foolish to leave Sweden without trying is *Filbunke med pepparkakor*, soft gingersnaps and clabbered milk (whole milk treated with a culture that makes it into something like a delicate yogurt). The best is supposed to be in the restaurant on top of NK department store, where it is also possible to order that other treat, *lingon i mjölk med knäckebröd*. *Knäckebröd* is the flat dry brown bread, like wafers. They are crumbled in a bowl of milk and sprinkled with the lingonberries. It's something eaten at home by every Swedish child and grown-up, and something everybody forgets to mention as a common Swedish specialty. The NK has lots of specialties on their menu, at low prices, and similar fare can be found in such restaurants as the Cattelin, Gondolen, Promenade, Regnbågen and Bäckahästen.

Nobody should leave Sweden without trying a *smörgåsbord*, although the Swedish admit that the groaning board is out of tune with modern times and has been overpublicized. Many of the restaurants have given them up because they are so wasteful, offering *assietter* instead, which is a plate of a few items, or *delikatassietter*, which is a plate of the more expensive ones. The restaurants do go all out with their Christmas tables, *Julbock* in the center, with the Christmas ham as the main dish, ten kinds of sausages instead of two or three, and a collection of special beetroot recipes. The *smörgåsbord* is approached successively, first the fish, then the sea food, then the cold meats, the hot dishes, and finally the cheese, followed by fruit and pastry. And the best of all is at Solliden in Skansen.

Skansen is a sort of park, zoo, and outdoor museum right in town, on the heights east of the city, easily reached by streetcar. It is full of ancient houses, animals, walks, and restaurants, the largest of which is Solliden, a dining room above an enormous outdoor café. All the restaurants are run by the same management, and after lunch you can wander around the park, buying hot dogs and hamburgers, waffles with cloudberry jam, cotton candy and coffee, fruit or soda pop, *tunnbröd* with fried herring or pork, and spitcake. *Tunnbröd* is the original of the crisp breads once baked in every Swedish home for Christmas. Spitcake is a dough dribbled on a spit that turns before an open fire to bake, and is finally dribbled with white icing. The stands are gathered into a row of stalls like a village market, and if you can't finish everything, there are the tame squirrels to help.

One reason for going to Sweden in the cold weather is goose, and another is duck. Chicken is often served with a cream sauce and rice, or fricasseed, accompanied with a compote of currants or other fruits, potatoes, and a creamed vegetable. But the goose is stuffed with apples and prunes, roasted, then served with poached cinnamon apples, stewed prunes, browned potatoes, and red cabbage. All sorts of delicacies are made out of the gizzards, liver, neck, fat, and skin. Ducks get similar royal treatment.

If you can't time your trip for cold weather, then try to arrive after August 8, which is the beginning of the crayfish season. Everybody goes on crayfish hunts and drinks *snapps*. They are eaten right through September, with bread and butter. There's another Swedish specialty, horsemeat, prepared I am told in many delicious ways. But I can't report on it, because that is not for me. Sorry to be prejudiced.

FINLAND

Finland follows the same Scandinavian pattern of glorifying fish, smoked meats, and the cold luncheon table, but the Finns eat later. They also have dishes that are com-

binations of foods like mutton and beef prepared together, *karjalan paisti;* or a pastry shell full of bacon, pork,
and freshwater herring, *kalakukko.* Like the Swedes, who
call it *strömming,* they prepare Baltic herring or *silakka*
in wonderful ways. *Keitetty kala* is pike simmered with
onion and allspice—a method used for preparing bass and
whitefish—and served with a dill sauce, or that Scandinavian favorite, sour cream in which there is some
horseradish. I think the names are great.

Something not to miss is porridge, made of various
grains, and eaten hot with a dab of butter and cold milk;
one of the best is barley pudding, *Uunipuuro,* which can
be served in place of potatoes. Beer and schnapps are
the popular drinks, but vodka is known, along with
various Finnish liqueurs, the most interesting being
Mesimarja and *Suomuurain.*

Helsinki is full of restaurants, most of them international, but generally showing a few local specialties to
please the tourists. The city is a summer resort, surrounded on three sides by beaches, but one of the best
times to be there is during the long spring. The country
has some 60,000 lakes, so trips to the countryside, and
picnics, are good ways to sample the smoked meats, fish,
and sausages. The Finns have the best architects in the
world, particularly when it comes to houses and apart-
ments, so plan your picnic near one of the developments,
just so you can see what can be done when people know
what they're doing.

GREAT BRITAIN

GASTRONOMY.   Solitary or surrounded, the English imbibe all manner of things in all manner of ways from all parts of the globe, at all times of the day or night, in all positions, for any reason from sustenance to sociability. Beginning with tea in bed before rising and concluding with a munch and sip before snapping off the bedside light, the time between is filled with food and drink, good and bad, native or foreign. Sweets are everywhere, beer and beef, fish and chips, whisky and wine, bread and jam, a vast and endless variety. The buffet, the teashop and coffeehouse, the pub or inn or tavern, the packet of sandwiches stuck in a pocket for a hike, the hamper readied for a drive, the tuck box sent to youngsters in school—all are English as marrow spoons, as tea cosies, as sugar tongs. No nation eats so casually, or so formally. Pleasures of the table are an answer to the climate.

BREAKFAST. Hot tea first thing, clear or with milk, and sugar, followed by a real breakfast that may include a boiled or coddled egg with ham or bacon, perhaps porridge or bread and jam, smoked fish or kidneys, sausage, and much more hot tea. For elevenses, the midmorning snack may be more tea and biscuits, a glass of sherry with a biscuit, even coffee.

LUNCH. Sometimes only a sandwich and a beer in the local, some prawns or fish or a stew in a wine shop, or a snap-up, or ready, dish in a nearby lunch counter, perhaps an omelet, or steak and kidney pie.

TEA & HIGH TEA. Tea is a meal, with sandwiches and cakes, usually, but high tea usually includes something hot—an egg or some simple savory dish, so that supper may be cold sandwiches or something left over. If lunch has been a hot meal at the club or a restaurant, tea may be just that, followed by a dinner with beer or wine. Or tea might be a banger and a pint, sausage and beer, at the local pub, when it opens.

DINNER. Depends on what you had for tea. Often a roast and vegetables after a simple tea, but frequently a meal of several courses.

SUPPER. A hot and savory dish if tea and dinner were light, or perhaps a sandwich and a beer, or maybe just a cup of tea, with biscuits, or cocoa.

STREET FOODS. Places to drop in have replaced the street barrows and carts, but on every side are teashops, pubs, fish-and-chip shops, and counter and stand-up eateries which concentrate mainly on sandwiches and cakes or pastries.

LONDON

The first time we went to England, a dozen years ago, we went almost unwillingly, dreading the overboiled vegetables drowned in water, the warm beer, overdone beef, rolls hard as boards crumbling to sawdust if you cracked them, dry cakes dissolving to sand in the mouth, full of hard raisins and smeared with sticky, sweetish, tasteless paste.

It wasn't Christmas, so there was no plum duff or God's Kitchel, or wigs and ale. What's Cornish clotted cream after *crème fraiche* in Normandy? Who cares about gooseberry fool and flummery, Melton Mowbray pork pies, and cheesecake like Richmond's Maids of Honor? Quince days come in October, the custard wind and pudding pies come during Lent. Who wants the English version of salami, of wurst, of *pâtè en croute?* So there's Dover sole and water-cress sandwiches and high tea. Who wants to eat badly for a week?

We ate in the pubs: good sandwiches, the beer was fine—and cheap. We visited cousins for a leg of lamb, nicely underdone, pan-roasted potatoes, garden salad and a trifle—at that time a week's ration of meat and eggs and butter, and very good, but we felt guilty. A wine merchant had us for an office lunch, but got mixed up and ordered cold platters for twelve at two instead of two at twelve—good, the smoked Welsh salmon and cold cuts and cheeses, but embarrassing. We went to Lyons'. My wife ordered bubble and squeak, and I had to order toad-in-the-hole. The waitress brought my wife cabbage and bacon, and me mashed potatoes with a couple of sausages stuck in it, brown gravy over all. OK. But it was years before I learned she'd made a mistake and really served me bangers and mash. A toad is sausage in a Yorkshire Pudding crust. A sausage by any other name ... Very English. Another wine merchant had us home to dinner, but it was French *filet*, followed by a homemade cordial that was too sweet to be believed. But outside of that cordial, which was good, I guess, we didn't have one bad thing in the whole week—everything grand, in fact, although we got a little tired of sandwiches, and ducked teatime.

Since, I've been back to Britain every other year or so, and never had a bad meal. But then, I've spent days in London, and never seen a fog, never even seen it rain, except for an afternoon sprinkle while the sun was shining. Fools and foreigners must get special care in England.

It used to make me mad when Europeans asked if it was really true that everything came out of cans in the United States, and "what does cottage cheese with half a peach and a maraschino on top taste like?" Everything's frozen now, and I haven't had it since schooldays, is my answer. But it rankles.

Not so with the English. A nation of leg-pullers, nothing seems to delight them more than to tell you about the awful meals they've had in England, as children in school, on the road, in famous restaurants, just last week. A cousin sent me a book of old English country recipes, just to prove how bad it could be. Raymond Postgate has done the British a great disservice by bringing out a restaurant guide for the British Isles, including Ireland, and keeping it up to date each year, so that it's now possible to find frankly edible food anywhere. The fact that the snob place in London right now serves horrible food, described to me as "foul, foul, foul," shows how far the English can go to discommode themselves; and right next door is a place that shows how contrary they can be— a pseudo Edwardian restaurant where the waiters dress in bowlers and look like Godot bums, and the food is not

bad...not really too bad...all right...in fact, quite
good.

London has a variety of restaurants as wide as New
York's, and a list from one person includes such varied
places as the expensive Parkes in Beauchamp Place
and La Rêve in King's Road, Luba's in Knightsbridge,
the Bistro Vino, the Troubadour, Ox-on-the-Roof, The
Antelope, the Establishment where you can watch old
movies while you lunch. A note says to visit the pubs on
the South Bank to get real London workingman's food. A
footnote adds that barbecued chicken is popular for late
at night when you don't know what you want; it's
called "mass murder chicken because it comes from South
Africa."

Everybody has his own list of pubs where the food is
good, unusual, or convenient, and every pub prides itself
on its own, special bangers, sausages which the English
use as interior armor plating to protect themselves from
the weather, visitors, an excess of pub crawling, or the
corrosive rigors of cocktail-party Martinis and Gin and
It, which is Italian vermouth diluted with gin, or the
other way about, depending on the party. Bangers can
be eaten with a roll, but it's more customary to chew one
down with half a pint of bitters. The English pride themselves on knowing sausage, and they make much of the
common food, as reverse snobbery or a way to wage war
against pretentiousness. There's one Londoner who delights in having business lunches at Claridge's, that pillar
of empire where service is still an art. He persists in ordering bangers and mash, ignoring the elaborate *plats* composed of delicacies gathered from the farthest reaches.

This poshery never fails to impress his companion, and he says that Claridge's do the dish remarkably well, but perhaps a spot too fancily.

There's no use at all going into much detail about London restaurants, when Postgate is available as a guide. Hotel food is often superb, and the best food in London is said to be at The Connaught Hotel, but everybody has his favorite. There's always the Savoy, and Overton's comes in for solid praise. There's Sheekey's for fish, and Wilson's, but there's also Bentley's with twenty-eight ways of preparing Dover sole, and Wheeler's, with its lobster soup. There's the Nosh Bar in Windmill Street for Jewish food, and the Guinea and the Piggy in Leicester Square for the name alone. So British. There's the Hostaria Romana in Dean Street for Italian food, but there's also Chez Ciccio. The Mirabelle in Curzon Street and A l'Écu de France in Jermyn Street are two of the dozens of good French restaurants. In London, as elsewhere, it's good to have friends to guide you, but Postgate is a substitute.

Roast beef. There's the Smithfield Restaurant and the Charterhouse in the Smithfield Market, there's Simpon's, the Baron of Beef in the City, and the first-floor restaurant in Scott's in Piccadilly. You won't get thick slices with a bone on, or a charred end piece, the way we can in the United States, for English beef is traditionally cut thin. Roast beef is regularly on hundreds of London menus, along with mutton from the South Downs or Wales, mutton pies, and steak-and-kidney pies. The mutton has a savor all its own, and is what we call lamb. Meat pies are made all over Britain, the most famous of which is probably Cornish pastry, a sort of turnover, to be eaten hot or cold. They are as much a part of English eating as bangers or tea. The Jolly shops have over a dozen kinds.

The clubs. Some of the best food in London is served at the clubs, all the more reason to have local acquaintances on the spot. Businessmen generally eat lunch at their clubs, and while the chefs pride themselves on their Continental cuisine, the English specialities are always there in season. There's nothing quite like sitting down and eating a curl of bread that's been dried in the oven, spreading it lavishly with country butter, and wondering if the summer whitebait from Greenwich is in season yet, or if it's too early for broad beans, to have with your mutton chop. Maybe a mixed grill would be better, with *mange tout*, baby peas cooked in their pods, and perhaps an English *profiterolle* for dessert, nothing at all like the French original, possibly better and certainly richer. Or maybe Somerset strawberries with clotted cream or scalded Cornish cream.

Maybe even better than the clubs and pubs for lunch is eating from the street stalls, particularly fish 'n chips in Chelsea. Fish and chips don't taste right unless they're sprinkled with vinegar and eaten from a cone of newspaper; the fish varies from season to season but whitefish is best, or maybe plaice, or rock salmon, more expensive than the usual cod, which is really best. There are the jellied eel stalls in Whitechapel—the most famous is Barney's in the East End near Aldgate—where little cups of green aspic are sprinkled with chili vinegar and spooned up between mouthfuls of bread and bites of pickled onions and cucumbers. There are also fish pies with mashed in other stalls, and baked potatoes called King Edwards, and boiled sea-gull eggs in the fishmongers in April.

Teatime. In all the hotels and countless restaurants. High tea is really early supper, just right before going to the theater, which starts at an ungodly early hour, eight o'clock. The place to go for tea is where all ordinary Englishmen go, which is home, but Lyons' is a home away from home, and a place not to be missed. Not that Lyons' is a place—they're all over London. Tea can be anything from just a cup of tea with milk, that's it, or can include a boiled egg, sandwiches, pancakelike crumpets golden with butter, cakes and cookies, toast and jam, maybe a meat pie or something else hot. After a big lunch, tea is just right for an evening meal, although many English households have tea, maybe even a high tea, an eight o'clock dinner, and then tea with a little something before going to bed. And tea first thing in the morning, of course, perhaps with a biscuit, an egg with bread and marmalade, then a real breakfast later, and then tea again for elevenses, or perhaps coffee and milk with something, particularly if breakfast has been light. No tea for lunch, of course, no one ever does.

The thrivings from the English countryside pour into London, and it's a pleasure to go to the markets to see what's arriving. Good places to eat all around the markets, and cheerful people to eat with, nighttimers having the last meal of their day with the dawn people having their second breakfast. There are many tourists that come to London and miss the markets, even passing up the flower market in Covent Garden. It is hard to understand why.

You don't have to go to the markets to see London's

edible horde. There's Fortnum & Mason, seven floors of pleasures from all over the world, but particularly from England and the Commonwealth—hams from Bradenham, York and Suffolk, Wiltshire bacon, back or streaky, and gammon, Cheshire cheese, Caerphilly from Wales, Stilton from Hartington and Melton Mowbray properly eaten in wedges, not with a spoon, Double Gloucester, Cheddar, Derby. For an eating tour of England, a trip to Fortnum's first floor and lunch on their top-floor restaurant will provide you with addresses enough for a year's tour. If you want still more, there's Paxton and Whitfield, right across the street, or Lyons' big supermarket at Cadby Hall, or D'Eath's near Victoria Station, or Harrod's, where the game, the meats, and the vegetables are a splendor. Eating in England can be glorious.

The wine-and-spirits trade more or less occupies a section near the vaulted cellars at the London docks, and while many travelers visit the ivory vaults and other bonded storage places at the docks, few ever get to see The Plain, where the wine butts and pipes are set for marking before being trundled to the cellars. It's worth trying to get a look at these, if you know somebody in The Trade, and it's even a pleasure to get a look at some of the ancient offices of the traditional houses. But failing that, there are the London wine merchants, the most famous of which may be Berry Brothers & Rudd, Ltd. or one of the shops of John Harvey and Son. There's a long list of wine merchants in the telephone book, and your hotel porter will suggest ones in your neighborhood. You may have trouble getting into the wine vaults at London Docks, but if you go to Bristol, Harvey's will welcome you gladly, having set up an

English country inn expressly for the purpose. It's one of the best places to eat in town.

A place that fascinates me is the Roses Lime Juice plant in St. Albans, the cathedral town that boasts of having the oldest inhabited licensed pub in England, the Fighting Cocks. It's amazing to me that England, which produces no limes, should be the home of the largest processor of a tropical fruit, for the limes have to come to Britain to become Rose's. The reason is that the English navy discovered a few generations back that limes prevented scurvy, and made arrangements with one of their purveyors to see that every ship in the British navy was supplied with lime juice, which is how tars came to be called limeys and their ships came to be called lime-juicers. The limes had to be shipped from the Caribbean to England for processing because the juice varied, according to one of the directors, "from season to season, from time to time, from lime to lime."

Consequently, seventeen thousand barrels of limes come to the London docks each year, to be taken by canal barge to Boxhead, where the juice is "polished" in a giant of a machine that consists of a great revolving drum coated with a thick pastelike filter through which the juice is forced. The entire handling is done by seventeen men, the juice then being sent to St. Albans for bottling. A lot of it goes right back to the Caribbean for use in gimlets, lime rickeys, Singapore Slings, and other refreshing British drinks.

Another engrossing plant is the Guinness Brewery at Park Royal, where Extra Stout, at 4½ per cent alcohol, and Foreign Extra Stout, a little over 7 per cent alcohol, are produced, with the aim that Guinness will taste precisely the same, wherever it is drunk. There was a great fuss when the plant was opened, because drinkers insisted that the London Guinness tasted unlike the true Dublin Stout, but all the hoohah died when the company admitted that London Guinness had been on the market for six months before the new plant was announced, and nobody had noticed the difference. The brewery was built at the insistence of the British government, which couldn't bear to see all those £.s.d. pouring into Dublin when it might just as well go into the pockets of the English. It was designed originally solely for beer production, all experimentation and research being carried on in the Dublin brewery, but that policy is now honored in the breach, and Park Royal is called the statistical department by company members, experimentation being constant, the enormous production considered simply a necessary distraction.

The plant is enormous, three great buildings linked together by pipes and passages. The entire process is nearly automatic. The place looks like a generating plant, a few men lolling round watching the conveyor belts and mash tuns and filling machines. The biggest department is the personnel department, the men properly deserving more attention than anything else around the place. For every pound spent on wages, there are ten pounds paid for materials and a hundred paid in duty, so the government is the most interested group concerned, except, of course, for the drinkers. All profits come from savings on loss, which is 6 per cent in most breweries, but only 3 per cent at Guinness, thanks to the scientists in the statistical department. The entire production is controlled from a single "mashing seat" in the great hall containing the caldrons in which the brew is made. The brewmaster makes his batches at three in the morning, carefully controlling the amounts of grain, hops, and water that go into the great vats. The mashing seat is surrounded by levers, and some people think it looks like a do-it-yourself electric chair and others think it looks like an automated throne. Everybody likes to squat in it for a moment, to get the feel of what it's like to control millions of gallons of Guinness. You're not allowed to touch anything, though.

The other breweries in England also welcome visitors, but inasmuch as breweries own all the pubs in England, they feel visits are somewhat of a waste of time when you could just as well be in the pubs, sampling the results. Guinness owns vast hop farms and a couple of hotels, but no pubs, and is glad to welcome visitors, but is loyal to the industry in being truly happy when you are busily consuming the fruits of the labors at Park Royal.

SCOTLAND

The Scotch distillers share the English feeling about consumption, but like the rest in the wine-and-spirits trade, they love to talk about their product. A good place to start is in Glasgow, the port from which much of the world's Scotch is shipped.

Glasgow is full of warehouses, many of them belonging to DCL, the Distillers Company Limited, which is a group that controls most of the Scotch distilleries. But the pride of the town is the new storage warehouse belonging to the largest of the independents, William Teacher & Sons, floor after floor of casks full of Scotch, sent down from the distilleries in the Highlands for blending and reducing. The malt whisky distilled in the Highlands is used to give body and substance to Lowland whiskies that have been distilled at high proof and aged for three or four years, so they have little taste. Glasgow water is excellent for reducing the blended whiskies to a drinkable proof, but it's too soft for mixing. The best water for mixing must have some character, like the water from which the Highland malts are made. Like tea, Scotch tastes different with every water used for mixing; London water is excellent, for instance, because it's full of calcium. In Glasgow, they say they like two things naked, and one of them is whisky, so they throw the Scotch down with a beer chaser.

Teacher's has a fine old office building in the main square of the town, where you can arrange for visits to their malt distilleries in the Highlands—Glen Rossie, Ardmore and Glendronach—and with the proper encouragement, one of the directors may see that you get a copy of an irreverent little book on the making of Scotch, with drawings by Ronald Searle. Up at the warehouse, they have an actual construction from one of the drawings, all lights and clanks and boggles, but this idiot still is usually off at a fair somewhere, beguiling observers.

You should have lunch across the way from Teacher's, in the St. Pancras Hotel, or up at the railroad station, in the Central Hotel. By avoiding the international dishes, you can get salmon from the famous lochs and rivers, leg of mutton, or smokies rizzarred on the rocks—haddock or mackerel or herring smoked over oak chips or birch or seaweed, but also partially air dried in the sun and wind, pressed between sods. You'll find smoked mutton hams, which you eat with bannocks or oatcakes, these last also being served with crowdie, the Scotch for cottage cheese. There's also cock-a-leekie, a fricassee of chicken and leeks, as well as barley broth, which is full of vegetables and mutton, this last being served separately, with neeps, or turnips. A side dish you should try is tatties and neeps, turnips mixed with boiled potatoes, and if you want something light there's Scotch woodcock, eggs scrambled soft in a double boiler and served on anchovy toast. The Scotch way is to use the yolks for the scramble, the whites for something else; it's often served as a savory, the British canapé, usually hot and always spicy, presented after dinner to clear your palate for the evening's drinking. And there's Scotch egg, a big sausage fritter with a hard-boiled egg inside, generally served with baked beans. If you'd like to make a lunch of smoked salmon or salmon mayonnaise, you might start with a hot soup like Brown Windsor, which is a staple of every hotel in the British Isles: "Everything's thrown in it, including the bacon rind and sausages left from breakfast," I was told by a disenchanted distiller. In any event, it's a wonder to see how the soup can vary.

The haggis is a rather innocent-tasting spicey sort of mutton sausage boiled in a skin, which is split open for eating. It's served with neeps and champit tatties, boiled spuds. The filling is mixed with oatmeal. It swells during boiling, and seems to continue to inflate after each forkful, so that the ball seems never-ending. Plenty of pepper is used for seasoning, so plenty of Scotch is needed while devouring. I'd prefer beer, but not in Scotland. Maybe haggis gets its awful reputation from its gray, irregularly globular appearance—it's sewed in sheep's gut for boiling, because you need something strong and expansible to withstand the swelling—and it looks for all the world like a primitive football that's been out in the wet too long. Maybe it's the idea of oatmeal in it, or the sheep's heart, lungs, and liver of which it is mainly composed. This is called the sheep's pluck, not too appetizing, but oatmeal is a common filling for minced-meat dishes, and the others aren't unusual.

I have my tasting notes from the first haggis I ever tasted. There are three separate entries: "a sort of mild meat stuffing...a drier sausage than a real *wurst*...a very concentrated food." You don't notice the pepper, at first. One haggis does nicely for two. I, for one, certainly intend to try it again. When I'm older.

Breakfast isn't to be missed in Scotland, not just because of the ham or bacon and eggs, the scones and Loch Fyne kippers or smokies, the marmalade or Robertson's Wild Brambleberry Jelly. It's the oatmeal that's best of all, traditionally eaten with butter and salt instead of sugar. A pitcher of hot milk or cream is often served with it, although these are sometimes cold, so you can dip your smoking spoonful into it for cooling.

Tea is the best time for crumpets and shortbread, Dundee cake and teacake. If it's a really high tea, you may have several kinds of scones, made from different doughs, with or without raisins. They are put on a girdle, which is the Scotch for griddle, and cooked before an open fire or in the oven—mostly the latter, these days—and cut in quarters for serving.

After tea, it's time for sweets. Edinburgh Rock; glessies, which are made from brown sugar and corn syrup, then allowed to harden, and smashed to bits; toffees of all

sorts; gundy, which is molasses taffy. Like the Irish, who
are also famous for their oatmeal, the Scots go in for all
sorts of chewy and sucking candies. Perhaps it's a way of
exercising the mouth so the language can be spoken, or a
way of limbering it up so that Scotch can be savored
properly.

Near Aberdeen is the town of Forfar, known for its
rocks, but also for Forfar Bridie, which is a mincemeat
pastry. The small meat pies of Scotland, particularly the
mutton pies, are gems in the Scottish crown, as is fish
baked in a custard; mince, which is a hash from beef; and
finnan haddie, made from smoked haddock from Findon,
near Aberdeen, the smoked fish being cooked with milk
and butter thickened with cornstarch and served with a
poached egg; a similar supper dish calls for more milk
and mashed potatoes with the haddie, to produce a soup
called cullen skink. What a name.

The place to have all these things, in case you missed
them in Glasgow, Edinburgh, or Aberdeen, is in the
Highlands. That's also the place for grouse and woodcock, trout rolled in oatmeal and fried, smoked sole for
breakfast, hot and golden on the plate, and perfect with
toast and tea. It might be an idea to pass through the cities
as quickly as possible, because most eating places there
serve Continental foods. It would be a shame to miss
Peter Evans Steak House, one of which is in Glasgow,
because they have fine Scotch steak, served with slices
of thin ham, or the Crammond Inn, just outside Edinburgh,
where the fish and the mutton are excellent, and you get
the feeling that you are playing a role in a modern English movie about the smart set. But better to miss it all
than to miss the Highlands, and the lochs, and the north
of Scotland. People are flocking to the cities and down

to England like lemmings, for no good reason, unless it's money and movies and motor cars, but those that stay behind have a fine, sparse, calm life in the wild country, where man has made his covenant with nature. Perhaps you have to love your woman and like yourself to stay there, and have a strong feel for the land and for the seasons. The bare low hills, scalped of trees for a thousand years, are spotty with yellow broom and gorse, brooks and wider streams meander through the glens, and it's here they make the true Scotch whisky, Highland pot-still malt whisky.

Nearly all the malt whisky goes to the blenders in the Lowlands, to give character to the brands that are so famous. Highland malt is too heavy in taste, it's said, to be popular with modern city dwellers, and certainly until the blends were first marketed over a century ago, Scotch was a Highlander's drink. Recently, there's been a growing demand for the pot-still malts from people who've decided the blends are too light in taste, and a few bottles find their way to the United States.

The most famous Highland malt is the Glenlivet, the first of the distilleries to make peace with the revenue collectors and pay the tax imposed. Its whisky is used in some of the most famous blends, but a little of it has traditionally been offered on the open market. One of the last of the independent distillers, the Glenlivet now sends a few hundred cases to us each year. Nobody knows why it should be the best, some insisting that it is the pot still itself that makes the difference, or the water, or the quality of the Scotch barley that is made into malt, or the way the peat smoke is used to roast the malt, or the skill of the brewmaster who decides what part of the run will be retained to age into whisky, the rest being returned to the next batch for distilling again. It is probably a combination of all these. So careful was one distiller not to change his whisky that when he needed a new still he had the old one reproduced exactly, dents, patches and all, so there wouldn't be the slightest chance for change. Distilling is done only in cold weather, the "silent season" beginning in May and continuing until October, but a distillery is still a splendid sight to see in summer.

Dufftown is the Scotch capital of the Highlands, and there are seven distilleries in all, most of the other famous ones being not far away. There's a hotel in Dufftown, but visitors who know about it like to stay in Castle Kildrummy, an hour's ride away. It's a new castle, built less than a hundred years ago, with scarcely a dozen rooms, so reservations need to be made well ahead of time. It is across the ravine from the ancient castle Kildrummy, where Robert the Bruce was betrayed to the English by one Osborne the Smith, who was promised all the gold he could carry if he showed the Sassenachs how to get into the besieged castle. He did, and the blacksmith was paid off in molten gold, poured down his throat. The old castle is a ruin now, but hundreds of trippers come to walk the stones, stopping for tea in the new castle, where they can get such things as Aberdeen butteries, and softies and syrup, as well as oatcakes and the usual teatime joys.

In the ravine between the two castles is a rock garden spread along the base of a cliff and around a lawn, with a path winding through it. It's a Japanese garden with a lawn for the pond and paths for the stream, laid out by gardeners brought from Nippon a couple of generations ago.

There's a funny sign in the garden which gets its message across: "Surely not in vain your cooperation ask? Leave the plants to grow and close the gates."

In the bottom of the glen is a stream dammed here and there to make waterfalls, emptying into a pond under a high-arched bridge. One of the sights is a cherry tree growing up through a millstone, and another is the calmness in the garden when the Highland winds roar the mists from the moors across the towering ravine, thrashing the trees on the rim.

In Dufftown are two of William Grant & Son's distilleries, another of the last remaining seven independent firms. They, too, have begun to market some of the Highland malt whisky, unblended, from their Glenfiddich distillery, reserving the malt from Balvennie for their own Scotch blends, Standfast and Grant's 8.

They are delighted to explain the Scotch-making process to you—how the dampened barley is laid out on floors to sprout, then how it is smoked on perforated floors to stop the germination, how it is mixed with water and yeast and allowed to ferment, then how the resulting wort is poured into the pot stills and the condensed steam collected. The clear liquid is placed in casks and the aging begins, eight to a dozen years for the full-bodied malt whiskies, and even longer—up to twenty and thirty years—for special whiskies. Four to six years is enough for many of the malt whiskies used in blends, although this requires distilling at a fairly high proof, so that smaller amounts of the highly flavorful impurities are condensed than would be the case if all the impurities were expected to disappear during the maturing process in casks.

Visitors are given tastes of the various whiskies, including some of those still aging in wood, and many's the person whose eyes fly wide at the first taste. Malt whisky is not heavy or oily, but it is very full in taste, and very pronounced. Perhaps not for everyday drinking, but then who wants to eat prime rib roasts all the time? The lucky ones get to buy a bottle or two, to carry away.

A list of the top distilleries would certainly include the following: the Glenlivet, Glenfiddich, Balvennie, Macallan, Cardow, Glen Grant; then there are the heavier whiskies from Islay, such as Laphroaig and Lagavulin, and those soft whiskies from Campbelltown, such as Glen Scotia and Springbank. The place to discuss their merits is in the Brewer's Office, the domain of the stillman who presides over the distillery and controls the runs in the stills. More than likely, he'll ask you if you'd like a dram to help the discussion along. Fools refuse.

To taste a variety of these whiskies isn't easy, in the sense that nobody is apt to have a collection, but a place worth trying is MacPhail's in Elgin, who deals in malt whiskies, selling them to the various blenders and on the open market. It is not prudent to taste too many, for it's apt to make you optimistic. After such a tasting, and in spite of all the miserable weather that's regularly expected in the Highlands, except, of course in summertime, I heard a previously dour Scotsman say, "It's been a fine day for several days now, I hope it will be a fine day through the week end, and I expect it will." But then he'd tried several drams of Glenfiddich at distillation proof, twelve years old, from a first dry-sherry fill. It was to be expected.

IRELAND

GASTRONOMY. Much fish and sea food, but many dishes are regional specialties that incorporate ham or bacon, potatoes and cabbage, as basic materials. Beef and veal are excellent, as are dairy products. Sweets of all sorts, beer, bread, and tea, are staples, but there is a profusion of sausages and other delicatessen. Poultry and dairy products are exceptional.

BREAKFAST. Irish oatmeal is rated with the Scotch and Dutch varieties, but bread and tea, with marmalade or jam, is a common breakfast. Smoked fish like kippers, bacon and eggs, kidneys, and other items we think of as part of the English breakfast, can be found anywhere.

LUNCH & DINNER. A perfect lunch is dark bread or soda bread, oysters, and stout, but most people have something hot, a fish or sausages or stew, served with potatoes. Dinner may be two or three courses, depending on what's for tea.

TEA. Generally bread and butter, some cakes or pastry, perhaps ham, cheese, and a coddled egg, with strong tea. Scones and crumpets are popular.

STREET FOOD. Street venders have pretty much disappeared, but the pubs and teashops serve sandwiches, sausages, an occasional hot dish, and a variety of pastries or delicatessen, varying with the sort of establishment. The pubs mainly concentrate on beer and talk, except at lunch, when there's usually a hot dish available.

Well, first of all you need to come to Dublin with the phew of beer on your breath, and if you're lucky and in an Irish plane it can be Harp or Phoenix or maybe Guinness, which is good for you. Right outside the airport is a billboard, big as billy-o, and on it's a lovely scene of a bit of Irish country, a lake and hills, and before this beauty is a great hand holding a foam-topped glass, and printed along the bottom in neat black type, it says, HAVE A WONDERFUL TIME IN IRELAND. What a fine way to welcome a man to a country, it is indeed.

A fine way to get to know a town—there's no better —is to walk the streets. It's a method not suggested for women alone, but what a way to find out what's in store. In the sweetshop windows there's raisin fudge which is red, elevens that look like chocolate marbles, liquorice allsorts and wilko japs, hazelnut whirls and peppermint crisps. There are pearl drops, which are tiddlywinks of white chocolate, honey twists, paradise fruits, cherry chips, and orange cracknels, there's the French mixture of marzipan roses and other shapes, and there's always Irish rock, a hard candy sold in chunks, and sticks called Peggy's Leg. The names may be better than the candies, but they make Dublin a children's heaven.

Then there are the snap-ups and the dellies, quick service snackbars and shops where you can eat at a counter or buy a bite to munch in Stephen's Green or out in Phoenix Park. Pork pies and sausage rolls, mince pies and steak and kidney pies, rollmops and frankfurter salad, breaded crubeen, that's pigs' feet and chicken cutlets, great rolled ox tongues and hams and pâtés.

The bakeries. There are baps, which are biscuits, and fadge, which is potato bread baked on a griddle; there are the round loaves called cobs; there's soda bread, and wheaten bread, which you eat with oysters or smoked salmon. There are the slabs of yellow cake—Madeira, marble, Dundee, which is full of dark raisins, seed, sultana (called barnbrack)—there are logs of all sorts, and fresh cream sandwiches—layers of cake separated with creamy fillings—there are chess cakes making yellow and chocolate square patterns when cut, sugar rings and sugar rolls, queen cakes which are yellow cupcakes, crumpets no bigger than a silver dollar and others an inch thick and four across, scones and tea biscuits, with or without raisins.

In the greengrocer's are strawberries from Tipperary, if you've timed yourself right to arrive in June, plums and raspberries, tomatoes small and red, and later on there are peaches and pears and apples.

Every country has its shops, but no place else is there such a musical lilt in the voices of those who are doing the buying. And when they tell you about a dish!

"There's yellowbuck, a lovely cornmeal bread, you can't get it any more, likely. Maybe in the country. It's gone, they say, because the English asked what made the Irish greyhounds go so fast. We feed 'em yellow-buck, says one, and now the English buy it all, but our dogs still win."

"Have you had pigs' feet and cabbage? You've not? There's a dish. From the south and west. Beautiful. A bit fatty, but it's very very nice."

"There's flannan bread. It's peculiar to Ring's End. Turns my stomach just to think of it. What you do is boil skate or ray. Then you cover a plate with stale bread and put the steamed fish upon it, and let it soak through. . . . It's savage, but there you are, it's a dish. . . . Oh Jaysus, God forgive them."

"Concannon. That's what they call it in the north, but down here it's calcannon. You boil the potatoes, and mash them with curly kale and onions. In Galway, they use parsley instead of curly kale and scallions for the onions. You simmer the scallions, and the parsley, too, if you use it. Down here it's with the kale, and you add cream or buttermilk. It's like champ, which you make with new potatoes."

"You know poundies? Mashed potatoes with butter, cream, and seasoning. But mind you whip it with a wooden spoon."

"Pratie apples. Slices on a triangle of potato dough, and you cover with another, squeeze the edges and cook it on a griddle. When they're hot you slit the top and slip in butter and sugar. My."

"You've had Irish oatmeal? You haven't? Have some."

"Bacon and cabbage, that's a country dish from the west. You simmer a piece of bacon until the skin is loose, then you put a bed of cabbage on the bottom and let it cook. It's better than corned beef."

"Coddle. It's streaky bacon or back bacon, cut into squares, boiled with pork sausages, onions, and potatoes."

"Poached salmon is the best. I always have to laugh when foreigners say poached salmon. The greatest poacher of them all when I was a girl in the west was Starry Ruant. They called him Starry because of all the freckles, a runt of a man. My father would meet him at the pub. Starry would wriggle up, something wrapped in paper under his coat, and say to my father, would you be likin' a nice fresh salmon, newly caught this very mornin'? They'd make the deal right there. Were they ever good!"

"Boiled spare ribs. You'd get up in the middle of the night to eat them."

"What's an Irish dish? Steak. And if it isn't steak, it's mutton."

"Have you tried the Featherbed? No, no. It's not a dish. It's a mountain near town. Lyable on. The local gazebo."

"I remember the first time I went to a meeting of the Oyster Society of Dublin. I got all dressed up. It wasn't that sort of thing at all. I didn't realize I was dressed like a dog's dinner. They don't let women watch the initiation ceremony. It has something to do with a goat. But they get a barrel of oysters and you eat them with stout and brown bread. I remember one man teased me. He said, 'Watch them. Just look. When you put the lemon on them, how they squirm.' The old fool. Pulling my leg like that. There's nothing on earth like Galway oysters. Thank God for that. And thank God they're seasonal, or Lord knows what we poor women would do."

The Irish have no great reverence for their food, and

the more they love it, the more they treat it lightly, rudely, roughly, mauling the dear wonders that delight their souls. There's no lamb in the world like Irish lamb, no mutton, no bacon, no brown trout or salmon, no butter or bread, no oysters. There are no prawns like those from Dublin Bay. No potatoes like Irish mealies. But an Irishman is never apt to say so, not directly.

The pubs aren't the best places to find out about Irish food. I don't mean you can't eat well in them, for there's nothing like a snap-up in one of the Mooney Pubs, and the smoked eel and roe are good, not just because they are new foods on the Dublin menus. I mean the talk about food in the pubs. Because the Irish tell you about food from their childhood, the wonders of the local dishes from Connemara or Clare, Sligo or Galway, and they are all spiced with memory and simmered in the stout. Home cooking and county cooking still make the best food in Ireland, a few say, when the cook is happy and the season right, a fact perhaps no truer in Dublin than anywhere else you might name. The warm and vivid Irish voices only make it sound much better.

As for pubs, Dublin is the place, and it's the Irish that make it so. They love the new audience provided by strangers, or so one is made to feel, and they listen as long as you have something to say, one is led to believe, and even if this is deception, charm and politeness mask the fact so that you have a good time. A good place to start a pub crawl is Bartley Dunne's, which isn't a pub at all, but a most popular place full of travel posters and bottles from everywhere in the world. It's a good place to start because the traveler learns at once that it's the people that make a pub, and this bar that wouldn't be out of place in Greenwich Village is the place to see a lot of the young business and theater crowd. It might be another one next season, but there will always be an Irishman to guide you.

There are at least a dozen pubs not to be missed in Dublin and here are seven to get you started: Davy Byrne's in Duke Street is modern now, and not a bit the way it was in Joyce's time; across the way is The Bailey, with a little counter restaurant downstairs, a big one up to the left, and the pub to the right, full of Trinity Students; The Long Hall Bar at 51 South Great George's Street is exactly that; The Brazen Head was once the hangout of highwaymen and revolutionists, but is now a place where you can hear the customers sing Irish songs; The Pearl Bar in Fleet Street is across the street from the *Irish Times* and often full of reporters, one of the most famous of which is Myles na Gopaleen, whose column has been called the best in the world. And there's Neery's in Chatham Street, the Stag's Head at One Dame Court. . . . You can find the rest by yourself.

There are the famous international restaurants in Dublin, Jammet's and the Russel and the Shelbourne, the Central Hotel, the Royal Hibernian, and Old Conna Hall in a luxury setting out in the country. The Irish cuisine at Coras Iompair Eireann, the exhibition hall in Dublin's Kingsbridge, is not to be missed. There's Beaufield Mews, which is an antique shop, the fish restaurant called The Red Bank. In Cork, there's the Oyster Tavern, and Godfroy's Hotel at Greenfields. But your best guide for all this is Postgate.

My favorite place is the Metropole in O'Connell Street, which is in a movie house. The big movie houses all have a variety of eating places in them—cafeterias, snack bars, tea rooms, lounge bars, and restaurants, and you choose one or the other, depending on what you want to spend and how you want to eat. Nobody interested in food would miss the Georgian Room in the Metropole, which specializes in Irish dishes and specialties from other countries. There's pork steak, for instance, stuffed with bread crumbs, onion, parsley, and sage, and another version that calls for nettle stuffing. There's a broiled ham steak with Irish whiskey sauce, and another version called ham Rosnaree that includes honey and Irish in the sauce.

Two other places not to miss are the airports, both Dublin and Shannon, which boast two of the finest cooks in Ireland, two of the finest kitchens, and two of the finest menus, both full of Irish specialties. Every other place, you may be tempted to head straight for town, but in Ireland take time to eat at the airport, on the way into the country and on the way out. Near Shannon is Bunratty Castle, where a 15th century meal is offered, part of a 24-hour stopover special that costs $15 and is a fine introduction to Ireland—and all of Europe, for that matter.

There are three spots that are not to be missed in Dublin, four if you're interested in Joyce, and go out to the Martello Tower, which is now a Joyce museum. You can see where he swam off the rocks, now guarded by a sign that says FORTY FOOT GENTLEMEN ONLY, and stand on the very spot where stately, plump Buck Mulligan rested his shaving mug. There's also available in the stores a map of Dublin showing the various spots frequented by Stephen and Leopold on Bloomsday, June 16, which happens to fall just before Irish Father's Day. In nearby Dalkey there's a good restaurant called The Guinea Pig.

But the three spots not to miss are Jamieson's Distillery, pronounced Jemmysons, and Power's Distillery, both of which will show you the distillery process and some of the old equipment now no longer used. The third spot is, of course, Guinness's Brewery, out toward Phoenix Park. Guinness is part of Dublin, and on the sides of all the busses you can read GIGFY—VG, and no Dubliner can fail to know what it means. Even the Pioneers, that distressing temperance group, knows what's good for them, even if they never touch it. Guinness stout is so made that it tastes the same everywhere in the world, and so that it will always pour just the right-sized head, no matter what container it come from—bottle, can, keg, or the new metal barrel, called an iron lung by the flippant. It requires no special handling, and the stout coming from it is called instant Guinness. The stubby bottles are called parish priests. Of course, the temperature must be right, never too cold, never too warm. Guinness is not just a a drink, but part of a way of life in Ireland, and while it may take you a dozen pints or more to find out why, there's no other way to even approach the Irish soul.

Other places you might not like to miss, in addition to the bulletin boards in the entrance of Trinity College— which can be more interesting than the Book of Kells in the library nearby, whose pages are turned each day by a certain Mr. Walsh—are the International Liquor Museum, beneath the restaurant in Kingsbridge Station, and the wine cellars of Robert E. Turbett & Sons. There aren't too many great cellars in Dublin, and they say it's because so many underground rivers run beneath the city, one of which is named The Poddle, and which is said once to have filled St. Patrick's Well. Unlikely as it may seem, soda water was invented in Dublin, in 1773, in an apothecary shop called Thwaite's, in South William Street. The company still makes soda water, but they no longer use the underground streams for a source of supply, which was once rumored to give it its special taste.

Dublin is full of underground currents because everybody seems to know everybody else, and to be interested. The city itself seems to be a sort of theater and the streets a stage, even though pubs take the place of sidwalk cafés, or maybe because of that fact.

The streets, for all the modern shops, seem to come from another time. You still see horses, for instance, for Ireland is still a horse country, about the only one left in Europe, and its studs provide mounts and drays for the rest of the world. The women, too, swing along the streets, sparkle-eyed and prancy, neatly heavy in the ham. People stand among the crowds offering bits of paper stuck with pins, "Help the animals, please help the animals," or maybe it's some other charity. Down the street is a man in a cap and baggy suit that's slouchy on him, strumming a mandolin with an up-down twang that lilts the melody. Down there is a violinist playing a whining song with a loud, long bow, dressed in a long gray coat and tight gray pants, high above thin gray socks and cracked black shoes. On the side street a black-suited, gray-braided old woman plunks "Danny Boy" on a yellow harp, a brown satchel beside her, a large conch inside it for the coins. Cropped girls clopping along on spiked heels hurry back to work, straight-backed women in dark suits, with furled unbrellas, hurry stiffly to the shops. It's breezy, bright with sun, cloudless, clear as a bell. Gulls mew overhead, one lights on a sill, limping along on the stump because he's lost a foot. A flurry of people rush out of Bewley's Oriental Café, rushed now because they sat so long over tea and cakes. It's Dublin in the afternoon, a fine place to be.

GERMANY

GASTRONOMY. The forests and farms of Germany, the mountains and coastal waters, provide the people with hearty fare made heartier by the German love of beer and dumplings, bread and sausages, game and wildfowl. The cold, damp climate whets hunger for the sweet and rich and robust, which in turn begets an appetite for salty, sour, and spicy tastes. Germany is full of orchards, so it's not surprising that fruits are often used with meats to make a sweetish sauce that contrasts with the spicy or pickling marinades often used for roasts and stews. Many of the old dishes, cooked long to produce dark, rich sauces, are still common in Germany. The variety of breads and rolls is vast, perfect contrasts to the wurst and cheese, the beer and flowery white wines.

BREAKFAST. Bread and rolls with jam, and coffee, are a common breakfast, although ham, sausages, and cheese are often added. English and American breakfasts are available in the hotels, as are fruits in season.

LUNCH & DINNER. Bread, cheese, and beer, often with ham, sausages, or other delicatessen—a German word —are common luncheon fare, augmented in cold weather with a hearty soup or stew. Fish and fowl are often eaten at lunch. Dinner is usually three or four courses, beginning with soup or fish, continuing with a roast of meat or fowl, and game in season, generally served with wines or beer. The beer halls and wine restaurants serve the whole range of German fare, so that dinner can begin with delicatessen and wine or beer, preceding a hot main course, and ending with dessert and coffee.

STREET FARE. Cafés offer delicatessen and sandwiches with tea, coffee, or beer, but most beer halls and wine restaurants now have stand-up counters or benches where barbecued chickens, sausages, stews, and various noodle and dumpling dishes can be ordered. Pastry shops and coffeeshops can be found in all cities, often enough combined with a restaurant or beer hall.

Eating is always a problem in Germany, depending on where you sit. Your host always prepares matters in advance, of course, but, as you approach the table, he changes his mind. There are too many tables pushed together, or not enough, they should go crossway, or maybe better up and down, you should sit in the middle, or maybe at the end, and the lady can't go there, but in the seat two places down, then Frau Doktor can go there, no, over here is better, and Fräulein had better go here, no, over there where I can look at her, ha-ha, I'll sit here, no, next to you, and the rest, oh anywhere, no, you'll be best there, you there, and the rest sit anywhere they like.

There's some reshuffling after everyone is seated, the table is moved back a little, or forward, or turned again, three people change once more, a chair is moved down three inches, then up one, and the host settles back to beam at everybody, nod to the waiter to bring the first course, and look hastily around for the captain who was supposed to have brought the beer and wines three minutes ago. Everybody may be in just the place that was originally intended, but the host has shown he's taking care of things, so that he is now free to plunge into conversation with his neighbors. Conversation is as important as food and drink, people at adjoining tables may become involved, and the talk is only interrupted, and that momentarily, to change plates and fill glasses. Sometimes the seating is prolonged, for others may get tired of being pushed around and do some rearranging on their own. Foreigners who dislike being chivvied may grab a chair in the midst of the swirl, even clutch a companion, sitting down firmly and clinging to the edge of the table so that it can't be moved any more. Tugs of war are usually spirited but brief. The host usually prevails, without demur from others, and at least one observer insists it's the way the young are trained to take orders, no matter how confused and nonsensical. It is mostly, however, an attempt to make every meal into a party, because the Germans work hard and long, and eating, drinking, and talking are a form of daily holiday. The same thing can happen when only a couple are involved, and a man alone may change from one side of the table to the other, moving it a little this way or that. But just when you are ready to make a trenchant generality about this cheerful custom, a party will sit down without a flurry. Germany has rebuilt itself in the past dozen years or so, and nobody is quite sure what's been made or what's to become of it.

Some things haven't changed enough to count, among them the bread and the beer, the wurst and the wine, the *Kraut* and the *Knödel*, all of which come in singular variety, to make a phrase. All German wine of quality is white, for instance, the best from the Riesling grape, but Rieslings from the Mosel, Rheingau, Rheinhessen, and Rheinpfalz are widely distinctive, just as is the sausage in different towns, or the dumplings, or the beer. Changes of this sort are what lend the German cooking its interest and excitement, along with such seasonal or regional specialties as asparagus or ham, fish or game. Other distinctions come from liking to combine fruits with meats, as they do in Scandinavia, and in the variety of soups and bakery cakes and cookies.

The part of Germany likely to be most familiar is the enormous port of Hamburg, which has had such close ties with England for so many centuries that strong tea is a favorite Hamburg drink. *Aalsuppe* is the most famous Hamburg specialty, but chilled fruit soups, *frische Suppe* made with breast of veal, vegetables, and dumplings, or *Arfensuppe mit Snuten and Poten*, pork parts in peasoup, are popular. Not exclusively Hamburg is *Frühlingsuppe*, spring soup with tiny vegetables, which is one of the finest dishes in German cookery.

There's *gefüllte Schweinsrippen*, pork chops stuffed with apples and raisins and rusks doused in rum, and *Holsteiner Würzfleisch*, kidneys and bacon with mushrooms in a paprika sauce. There's *Labskaus*, sailor's beef, pickled brisket, and herring mixed with mashed potatoes and served with pickled beets and cucumbers, and the *Sauerbraten*, which should be marinated for several days, is as good as in its home country in the south. Fish of all sorts, particularly cod, is outstanding in Hamburg. It's a sailor town, and after a startled evening in the wild nightlife section called the Reeperbahn, a good place for an early breakfast is the Sunday morning market at Landungsbrücken, which is as weird as the Reeperbahn is bawdy, with hawkers wandering between the stalls and the nightlife continuing in the dance halls to a corny sailor music called *pankaken Kapelle.*

Nearby Bremen is even more international than Hamburg, being the port used by the wine trade, and full of old inns such as the Ratskeller and the Essighaus, where you can get *Kükenragout,* chicken, mussels, and sweetbreads, asparagus and peas, in a cream sauce; *Braunkohl mit Pinkel,* kale with groat-and-bacon sausages, which is the subject for a great autumn feast day; and *gepflückte Finten,* which is a dish of green and white beans, carrots, and apples. All of these can be washed down with *Kornbranntwein,* a clear schnapps made from wheat, locally called *Doornkaat* or *Söpke* and supposed to be excellent after fatty foods.

Down in Hannover, to the south of the Lüneburger Heath, you get *Grünkohl mit Brägenwurst,* which is curly kale with another kind of sausage, and so it goes through Germany, kale becoming cabbage, red, white, or green, and one wurst after another. Here the local drink is *Lüttje Lage,* beer and schnapps together, which is also popular in nearby Braunschweiger, from whence first came the famous liverwurst. The locals hold out for their own *Ahrbergs Bockwurst* and *Eisbein und Sauerkraut,* pork and you know.

Prominent in Hannover are the Sprengel Chocolate works and Bahlsen Keksfabriken, which has just about the biggest and most up-to-date cookie factory of modern times, like something out of Chaplin's movie of the same name. The machines are tended by some six hundred imported Spanish girls, housed in barracks nearby where they live in pairs, something Charlie Chaplin never thought of. There's a fine smell over all, and it's a sight to see the great machines making, for instance, sugar-cream wafers, the tops coming down from on high, the bottoms up from below, squeezing gently against an oozing center. Nobody's allowed to smoke around the place, not even the directors, because tobacco taints the butter. Bahlsen's is the most famous cookie factory in Germany, priding itself on using only natural materials.

At Hannover is made that honey liqueur, Bärenfang, which originated in East Prussia, but moved right after the war, and in the rolling country to the south is the little town of Steinhagen, where is made the juniper schnapps that goes so well with the local Westphalian ham, black bread, and radishes. This gin lunch is shown on the label of the stone crocks, called *Keucks*, used by König for shipping their *Schinkenhäger* gin around the world. Leave out the radishes and you have breakfast. The bread on the label isn't pumpernickel, but black bread from coarsely ground grain. Pumpernickel is full of whole rye grains, and *Kommis* is a similar dark rye used in the army. Each has its own taste, and black is best. Other local schnapps are Wachholder, Doppelkorn.

Just to the west, Münsterland Korn is favored with the Westphalian ham, along with the cheese and *Bauernbrot*, peasant bread, baked in a stone oven over birch logs. With beans and bacon, or pea soup with *Mettwurst* (mostly pork), or the local stews, Munster ale might be preferred, along with *Knabbeln* or *Stuten*, chunks torn off a loaf of newly baked white bread, then rebaked and kept to age for a time. Or, because Dortmund is the capital of Westphalia, one of the famous beers like Dortmunder Union might be drunk. Still further south is Düsseldorf, known for its cheese sandwich called *Halwe Hahn*, and a good place to try it is Zum Urigen or one of the other *Brauerei* in town, most of them operated by breweries. Schiffchen is a typical restaurant where you might get the Köln beer specialty, double fermented *Kölsch* or *Wiess*.

But forget beer, for southeast lies wine country, along the Rhine and its tributaries, the Mosel, the Nahe, and the Main. There's *Rheinsalm* and *Forelle blau*, and *Moselhecht*—Rhine Salmon, blue trout, and pike from the Mosel —not to mention the game from the hills. The storied Rhine begins just upstream from Köln but the glorious vineyards don't start until you get past Coblenz, where the Mosel flows into the Rhine.

The Mosel is one of the five or six most beautiful places where great wines are made. The river starts out high in the French Jura, meandering north to the border until it reaches Trier, where it begins to loop and twist northeast to Coblenz, straightening itself out again before pouring into Father Rhine. The great wines come from vineyards on south-facing slopes in the loops between Trier and Traben Trarbach, half on one side of the river, half on the other. The towns are full of small hotels and inns, among them the Schwarze Katz, in Zell, named after a famous but small wine, smaller than the hotel, which has perhaps twenty rooms.

Driving up the valley from Coblenz, you begin to get

the look of medieval and Romanesque Germany at once;
the market place in Kobern, the castles in Gondorf, Al-
ken, and Moselkern, particularly Eltz, the monastery
town of Treis, the medieval half-timbering in Cochem
and Beilstein, where so many German films have been
made, the market in Wittlich. Maybe the best way to
see it is to rent a boat in Trier and float down the river
for a few days, stopping when you're thirsty, camping
on the banks. On summer mornings the water is filled
with tiny bubbles and the people say even the river
blooms. The slopes are white with apple blossom in early
spring, and in May the terraced vineyards bloom. When
the frost hits in September, the steeps are bronze and
gold. There are vintage festivals in the towns, and in
Bernkastel the fountain runs with wine.

The towns with the finest wines are Erden and Ürzig,
Zeltingen and Wehlen, Graach and Bernkastel, Braune-
berg and Piesport, but there are lots of others, and the
names are easy to remember after tasting the wines. The
best wines bear vineyard names, and these become easy
to remember, too. Trier is one of the oldest German
cathedral towns and St. Matthew is said to be buried
there. Nearby is Neumagen, the oldest wine-growing site
in Germany, boasting a Roman wine ship and a song
called "Mosella," written by the Roman poet Ausonius.
The Saar and Ruwer flow into the Mosel near Trier. Both
of them are wine valleys, producing incredibly light and
delicate wines in good years, which are called Sonnen-
feuer, Sternengold, Kühler Mondlichtschein.

Across the Hunsrück, the protecting hills to the east,
is the valley of the Nahe, flowing parallel to the Mosel
and reaching the Rhine at Bingen. The hills are full of

game, the river slopes are lined with vineyards, and in the little village of Idar-Oberstein you can get *Spiessbraten*, beef roasted on the spit the way it's done in Brazil, a craft brought to the old country from the New World by polishers of precious stones, who first came here to make jewelry from the local agate.

The greatest German wines come from the Rheingau, on the hills opposite Bingen, a string of towns full of inns and surrounded by vineyards. Their names are known around the world: Rüdesheim, Geisenheim, Johannisberg, Winkel, Hallgarten, Östrich, Hattenheim, Erbach, Kiedrich, Rauenthal, Eltville, Hochheim. The English call them "hocks," from the last-named town, and, like the best of the Mosel, the wines are made from the Riesling grape.

The ones to drink are those with vineyard names, preferably including the name of the grower. Those marked *Spätlese* are made from late-picked grapes and are fuller and richer, but not necessarily sweet, and those marked *Auslese* are made from specially selected bunches, and are still fuller, even perhaps slightly sweet, so that they would be good with fish or pork. There are very expensive wines called *Beerenauslese* and *Trockenbeerenauslese*, from selected grapes, and from selected dried grapes, but these wines are sweet and luscious and rare, meant to be drunk by themselves when you want to have something extravagant.

The most interesting of the hotels is Die Krone in Assmannshausen and high above on the Niederwald is a former royal hunting lodge that is now an inn, reached by a cable railway that swings above the vineyards, as well as by a road. In Rüdesheim is the *Drosselgasse*, the thrush's alley, lined with wine taverns where tourists sing old drinking songs sitting at bottle-filled tables, swaying with linked arms in time to the tune. The town also boasts the most important and one of the handsomest distilleries of German brandy, Asbach Uralt, an excellent place to begin a tour of the town.

Back in the hills is Kloster Eberbach, once a great Cistercian monastery and now the headquarters for Rheingau vineyards owned by the state. A restaurant now occupies the former gatekeeper's building, and one can order a plate of cold cuts and a bottle or two, sitting under the trees looking across a duckpond to the orchards and walled vineyards. It is a serene place to have lunch.

The river Main empties into the Rhine at the eastern end of the Rheingau, and on the left bank is the cathedral city of Mainz; with its wine firms and its wine museum, it is the capital of the Rheinhessen, whose soft, full wines come from vineyards to the south. The most famous of all German regionals, which are blends of wines from a particular district, is Liebfraumilch, which has borrowed the name of wines originally produced in vineyards surrounding the cathedral at Worms, the Liebfrauenstift. The vineyard wines are much better than those simply called Liebfraumilch. The best wines of Rheinhessen come from the towns of Oppenheim, Dienheim, Nierstein, Nackenheim, and Bingen, and if you say them fast it sounds like a law firm.

Just south of Worms begins the district called the Palatinate, or the Rheinpfalz, whose wine towns are joined by a road sensibly called the Weinstrasse. The good vineyards are all in the Mittelhaardt, which begins near Bad Dürkheim, which boasts the world's largest sausage festival, as well as Germany's greatest wine festival, in September or October. Best wine towns are Wachenheim, Forst, Deidesheim, Ruppertsberg, and Königsbach. The climate is so mild almond trees and palms grow in the gardens. Perhaps the prettiest town is Deidesheim, which is tunneled with wine cellars. It has an excellent inn, the chair backs of which bear crests from famous vineyards. You can try going from chair to chair, drinking *Schoppen* of the wines in turn, but it might be better to have *Püffchen,* which are half-glasses. In Bergzabern, to the south, is one of the finest old inn buildings in Germany, and across the Rhine in Heidelberg is the Heidelberg Tun, the world's largest wine vat, a student restaurant called the Mensa in one of the few remaining Renaissance buildings, and a handsome wine garden and restaurant attached to the baroque Kurpfälzisches museum.

Up the Main is Würzburg, the main town of Franconia, which is famous for its Frankenwein, often called Steinwein, after a famous vineyard nearby. The wines are mostly from the Sylvaner and Traminer grapes, and from the Müller-Thurgau, a cross between the Sylvaner and Riesling.

To the south is Stuttgart and the Black Forest. Wines are made everywhere along the Rhine in southern Germany, but the *Schwarzwald* is most famous for its fruit distillates, aged in crocks and colorless. *Himbeergeist* is made from raspberries, *Kirschwasser* from cherries, and others marketed under the French names are made from strawberries and plums. There's one with gold flakes that originated in Danzig, called Goldwasser, which is still to be found. These are afterdinner drinks, but before dinner it's the wine, a bottle or two to whet the appetite, or perhaps one of the wine bowls: *Maiwein* in the spring, steeped with *Waldmeister* (woodruff) and full of strawberries; in July is the *Pfirsichbowle*, with peaches; and any time is time for *Kalte Ente*, cold duck, made by pouring white wine and the sparkling wine called Sekt over sliced lemon and some Curacao.

Nearby is Frankfurt, with its many cafés and its original hot dog, its bakeries, and the fascinating market called the Fressgasse. Across the Main from Frankfurt is suburban Sachsenhausen, where there are the Äppelwoi inns, *Woi* being cider, which is considered good with such wursts as *Fleischwurst, Gelbwurst, Zeppelinwurst,* strong *Rindswurst* and *Schwartemagen*. The *Brezel* girls wander around selling pretzels, *Kümmelwecke,* and *Hartekuchen,* biscuits to make you thirsty, which taste good with *Handkäse mit Musik,* if anything does, a rightly abused strong cheese mixed with onion and vinegar and oil that Germans seem to persist in eating out of contrariness. The favorite dish in Frankfurt is probably *Rippchen,* pickled pork ribs, or maybe it's *Solberflaasch mit Sauerkraut,* pigs' knuckles. Something particularly liked is *Grüne* sauce, hard-boiled eggs mashed with fresh spring herbs.

Over east is Munich, the beer capital of the world, with the scientific beer school in nearby Weihenstephan. There's the famous Restaurant Waltherspiel in the Hotel Vier Jahreszeiten, the Ratskeller in the town hall, almost as good as the one in Hamburg, and hundreds of others, but there are two places not to be missed.

One is the largest restaurant in the world, which can handle five thousand at a time, a series of rooms, including beer halls, called Mathäser. There is food at all prices, depending on the type of service you want, everything from sausages at a stand-up counter near the entrance to tables with flowers in a private room where international specialties can be ordered. No matter where you go most people order *ein Helles,* a lager, although some insist on ordering *ein Dunkles,* the dark beer, particularly in winter.

The second is Hahnhof, run by a wine firm from the Pfalz, which produces not only the wines for the restaurants, but everything else, from butter to wurst, on its own farms. There are four Hahnhofs in Munich, as well as ones in Frankfurt and Heidelberg, but the one that's biggest is in Eisenmannstrasse. They, or the beer halls, are the places to order a *Schlachtplatte,* which is the German version of a mixed grill, naturally including sausages. The plates of bread and cold cuts, the roast suckling pig called *Spanferkel,* the *Reh,* or venison, all are excellent. Afterwards, it's time to go to Schwabing, the nightclub center that is also full of students, a sort of German Greenwich Village, and at dawn there's time to go to Donisl's for white sausages. *Weisswürste* are unsmoked and simmered in water; they are a breakfast sausage, but they are also served in mid-morning, with dark bread and beer. If you want something more full of taste you might try the hot liver paste dish called *Leberkäs,* served with beer, of course. As for beer, the Weissbeer that originated in Berlin is popular, often served with a slice of lemon, or a dash of raspberry or strawberry syrup, said to be delicious on a hot summer afternoon.

Well, you can't miss Munich, and you can't miss the Mosel, and there's Würzburg, and the country around

Hamburg, and Lake Constance, and the Rheingau, and all those sausages and soups, all the breads and pastries. But there's no point starting in again. Just be as cheery as you can in arranging the seating at table, and always grab the prettiest girl to sit beside you, to explain the German slang as it flows along, and to help you with the beer and wine.

AUSTRIA

GASTRONOMY. Pastry is exceptional in Vienna and the coffeehouses and bakeries serve all sorts, with strong, black coffee and whipped cream. Boiled beef and *gulyás* are served in various ways, the *gulyás* being various forms of Hungarian stews. Austrian cooking is similar to German cuisine, with much pork and delicatessen, but many dishes come from Hungary and the other central European countries, from Alpine cookery, from Greek, Italian, Turkish, and other eastern Mediterranean cuisines.

BREAKFAST. Coffee with cream, or chocolate, with various breads or rolls, and sometimes an egg. English and Continental breakfasts are served in the hotels.

GABELFRÜHSTÜCK. Midmorning snack in a restaurant or coffeehouse, usually a beer and a sausage or small serving of *gulyás* or boiled beef.

LUNCH. Sometimes a light but expanded version of the midmorning snack, but often fish, an omelet, or a stew, generally with dumplings, accompanied with beer or a light white wine. Alternately, delicatessen in a *Konditorei* or bakeshop.

JAUSE. Midafternoon snack, usually cakes or pastry with tea or coffee, in a coffeehouse or bakeshop.

DINNER.   Usually a meal of at least three courses, often
soup or fish followed by a meat or fowl dish and dessert,
with wines or beer. Game and wildfowl are popular.

STREET FARE.   Sausage stands abound, but the Viennese
regularly drop into a coffeehouse, brewer's restaurant,
or bakeshop for delicatessen or pastry.

Getting to know a city is like falling in love. You're aware
of a hand on your arm, a shoulder brushing against you.
An odd turn of phrase surprises you, a quick laugh warms
you. You're in love again. It happens to a traveler all the
time, if he waits long enough, if he gets around, if he
keeps his heart out. And it can be a place, as well as a
girl.

I arrived in Vienna one windy spring day when it was
50° and cloudy. It began to rain as the airport bus joggled
into town. No porters. The taxi driver had a cold and so
did the lady who ran the little hotel I'd been misdirected
to; the sheets were clammy. Next day was Sunday and
in the rain I took the tour to Schönbrunn, listening to the
guide complain about last year's Brinkley show that had
poked fun at the quantities of whipped cream gobbled in
Vienna and the casualness of workers. I sat alone in a
couple of modernistic coffeehouses, I had drinks in the
bars at Sacher's, the Bristol, and the Imperial, listening to
the tourists, took a cab to Fatty's, the jazz place, which
was deserted when I got there—too early—and went my
rainy way to bed, between the still clammy sheets.

Monday, I was to go up the Wachau, and had to catch
a seven o'clock train, skipping coffee at the pension be-

cause it was very early, and because I didn't know it was included. But there was no restaurant open at the station. Outside, there was a stand selling *Wurst* and I stood in line to buy one. People scurried by on the way to work. Everybody seemed to be carrying bunches of lilacs, tulips. A weak sun shone on the streets, not enough to light the people. The man slapped a big, fat sausage on a piece of paper, a dollop of brown mustard, and handed me a roll. I had to juggle to pay him, and finally took a bite, dreading the greasiness, the lukewarmness, the sogginess of the roll, the too-sharp bite of the mustard.

The sausage was hot and juicy, just spicy enough, slightly smoky and sweet. The roll was crisp, the mustard just hot enough to match the spiciness of the *Wurst*. Best breakfast I ever had. I love Vienna.

A *Wuerstelstand* is at every busy intersection in the Ring—that wide circle of boulevards named the Ringstrasse that surrounds the old city—except where the surroundings are too fashionable to tolerate anything so common. If only they served beer. But you have to go to the restaurants for that.

The Viennese have an ancient reputation for being great snackers. All the restaurants serve *Gabelfrühstück*, not just for those who missed breakfast, a light midmorning meal practically designed to be served with a beer —a *Wurst* or two, a small serving of beef or veal *gulyás* (we call it goulash), some Beuschel, which is minced lights with dumplings, or a little *Beinfleisch*, boiled beef with horseradish. The horseradish is often mixed with cream or applesauce, and is another reason for falling in love with Vienna.

If the sausages don't do it, or *Gabelfrühstück*, there's

Jause, an afternoon snack, any time after three in a *Konditorei,* the Viennese pastryshop that's a combination of bakery, confectionery, and delicatessen. From the cases and long tables you can pick what you like to stay you until dinnertime, a beautiful bit of this or that to have with tea or coffee. Pastries are the main attraction—like *Sachertorte,* the chocolatiest of layer cakes, or the mochas or white cakes decorated with purply candied violets and other sprigs and sugary dices in rococo patterns. *Indianer Krapfen* are chocolate puffs filled with whipped cream; there's *Guglhupf, Buchteln,* various kinds of *Strudel* (get somebody to tell you how the pastry is supposed to be stretched out thin on a round marble table until you can see through it, so that when it's folded there are many layers of flaky air enclosing the juicy apple or plum inside). A wise and slim sweet-tooth ought to allow a fortnight for sampling the Viennese *Konditorei.* The weak and plump should plan an active schedule. Here's the place to try hot chocolate with whipped cream, although the pastries *mit Schlag* are most sensible with strong, black Viennese coffee or tea and lemon. The most famous *Konditorei* is Demel's, too conveniently close to the famous shops of the Kohlmarkt, but there's also Lehmann's on the Graben, the Gerstner or Heiner on the Kärntnerstrasse, and hundreds of others outside the main shopping districts.

Still, the best thing in all Vienna is the coffeehouse, all shapes and sizes and styles of rooms with all sorts of tables and booths and benches. Tourists like me love them for breakfast—if you can find a place where it's not included in the price of the room—where you get a basketful of rolls, some paved with poppyseeds, and slices of *Kaiser-*

semmel, a slightly sweet bread often full of raisins, with saucers or pots of marmalade and jam, butter curls if you ask for some, and a steaming pot of coffee, spiced or unspiced, or chocolate. *Schlag,* of course, if you want it. The hotels serve the same sort of breakfast, tossing in a boiled egg, or whatever, if you ask, but don't include the two glasses of water.

In the coffeehouses, even if you just order coffee it's always served on a small tray, with two glasses of water. Vienna was famous for centuries for the best water in Europe, from cold springs high in the Schneeberg and Hochschwab, sixty miles away. The Americans ruined it after the war, in their oversanitary way insisting on loading it with chlorine, but as soon as they left, the Viennese reduced the stinking chemical so that it's not noticeable, and it's again the delight it used to be. Just right when you don't want a third pot.

It's not the looks or the coffee that makes a coffeehouse a haven, or even that the waiters are adepts at choosing a paper or magazine in your native tongue to bring you as they come to take your order. It's that they like to have you there, whether you order more coffee or not. The first pot is a ticket of admission to the club. You can sit there all day if you want, reading all the periodicals, writing letters, reading a book you've brought, studying maps and tourist pamphlets, or just watching the girls go by or flirting with the one across the room who pretends to be deep in her own literary fare. When waiting or in doubt in Vienna, you go to a coffeehouse. Everybody has his favorites (I like Landtmann's), and favorite times of day (I like mornings before eleven, afternoons after four, and evenings after eight). The theater people, the artists, the writers, all have their favorites, which change somewhat with fashion, so you need to inquire after you arrive.

The coffeehouses were almost done in after the war, when espresso machines became the rage, and espresso bars sprang up all over the city to attract the young and jukey. The owners were quick to install the hissing monsters, and the Viennese were quick to realize that it wasn't the coffee that made the coffeehouses, which took a new lease on life. They'd always served food, but the espresso craze pushed the coffeehouse chefs to greater efforts, particularly in producing Austrian specialties, and they now serve some of the best meals in town.

Tourists almost ruined the restaurants, which had come to catering to the steak-and-chicken elite, and to the international passion for French and exotic dishes. By 1956, local specialties had become so submerged that the association of hotel, restaurant, and café owners, HORECA, got together and decided that they ought to feature at least one Austrian specialty on every menu every day. They inaugurated a Viennese Culinary Feast the first two weeks in June, to run during the Festival of Vienna. The visitor gets a card, which is punched each time he orders a specialty in one of the restaurants, and when he's been punched six times, the owner bustles up with a drink, a souvenir, and a certificate denominating him a "Gourmet Viennois." As you can see, the French influence is still much too strong, but the owners tell you that the name sounds better than "*Wiener Feinschmecker*," which is a point. Anyway, you can now get Viennese specialties in all the good restaurants all year, and in all the cheap ones, naturally. Even those that don't take part in the gastronomic "do," and insist on concentrating on international and classic dishes, serve regional food. One of the best of these restaurants is the *Drei Husaren*, which would be outstanding anywhere.

Nobody in his right mind needs a week to fall in love with Vienna. There's the Prater and its Ferris wheel and scenic railroad and *Wurstelständen*, the Schönbrunn palace, the Opera. This you have to get tickets for ahead of time, unless you want to stand in line with the students, working your way through the corridors and up the stairs finally to reach the lounge, where you can get a fine ham sandwich and a bottle of beer to hold you until after the performance, when you can go to the most famous hotel in Vienna, Sacher's, right behind the Staatsoper, with its maze of different eating rooms. There's the Spanish Riding School, the Wienerwald to walk and picnic in, all the museums, and the greatest glories of the *Barock*, especially the masterpiece of the most famous of the baroque architects, the Karlskirche of Fischer von Erlach, and the Belvedere by that other master, Johann Lukas von Hildebrandt. Even the clouds are *Barock* in Vienna, billowing like whipped cream over the park-filled city. And what's more, there's the Nineteenth District and its *Heurigen* (wine taverns) just a streetcar ride away. The Viennese have been brilliant enough in this day of depressing city planning to keep and modernize their trams, and the best place to go on one is the Grinzing. You catch trolley #38 at the Schottenring. When you arrive, you'll see above the winehouses a clock with no hands, fitting for those about to drink the young wines.

The *Heurigen* are strung along the wide street at the

end of the line, and there are others in the neighboring suburbs of Nussdorf, Sievering, Heiligenstadt, and Neustift am Walde, all conveniently near the Vienna Woods, which is perfect for dawn didoes. The young wine of the previous vintage is the cause for all the attention, but *Alter* from earlier vintages is also served, by the glass, pitcher, or bottle—inside when the weather's cold or foul, outside when the nights are clear and warm. The middle-aged and middle class used to be the ones to fill the gardens, arriving loaded down with hampers of food, to listen to the strolling violins and accordions, and join in the singing, but today the young people and the smart set add to the warm-weather throngs. Some of the houses are innlike and *gemütlich*, others are modern or plushly Empire, but all of them are cheerful, with roaring fires in the winter. Those that are open hang out a vine wreath or a bush on a pole, still the custom in rural Austria to announce that wines are being served. Some of the wreaths are so faded and battered that you'd think the places never close, and many don't.

In 1760, Maria Theresa instituted a law that only cold dishes could be sold in the *Heurigen*, and it was the custom to bring your own, or buy fancy box lunches from Demel's or Sacher's, but by 1958 the tourist pressure was so great that it was decided to permit the serving of hot food and now you can buy smoked ham or *Wurst* and sauerkraut and other specialties, as well as all sorts of cheese and delicatessen. Or you can just drink the wine with *Brezels* or a plate of black bread, which you sprinkle with salt. Just right with the special music called *Schrammel*. Any moment you expect the Student Prince to appear, or at least a Biedermeier girl, complete with ringlets, off-the-shoulder bodice with puff sleeves, and full skirt. But modern girls in their perky fedoras suit the setting, too, and there's always a dirndl or two, on the waitresses or the tourists.

Vienna wouldn't be the same without *Tafelspitz* or *Beinfleisch,* the two most typical ways of serving boiled beef, and *Geselchtes,* which is smoked pork served with sauerkraut and the big liver dumplings called *Leberknödeln.* Like the sausages and other smoked meats, these taste best with beer, the three favorites being Liesinger Bier, Schwechater Bräu and Gösserbräu; this last brewery operates several restaurants in Vienna. And several places feature the famous Salzburg beer, Stiegl Bräu. The light and stealthy white wines seem to go better with the famous Viennese breaded dishes: *Wiener Schnitzel* (*Holstein* means the pounded veal scallop is served with a fried egg); *Gebackene Leber,* which is breaded calf's liver, and *Backhuhn,* which is breaded fried chicken. *Brathuhn* is grilled chicken, and *Masthuhn* is baked chicken, often in a casserole with a crumb or pastry crust. All of these are served with tiny noodles called *Nockerln,* which also appear in soups and sauces. Along with such game as wild boar and venison, and various salads, there are all sorts of specialties of veal steaks with various sauces, and ham and pork dishes, all of which you can find listed as specialties in the list of restaurants published by the tourist office in connection with the June Culinary Feast. Not to be outdone by the *Konditorei,* there are various famous desserts employing eggs, including *Palatschinken,* which is a jam-filled omelet, *Kaiserschmarrn,* which is a sugared omelet torn apart with forks, and *Salzburger*

Nockerl or *Schneeknödel*, which is a foamy baked mound
of eggs whipped to peaks, sugary and golden on top, an
alp of froth, a baroque soufflé. In one of the old taverns
in a Vienna side street, I watched the faces of two
youngsters having their first lunch out with their parents,
and their first *Schnee*. Nothing could show better the
wonder of the dish.

The old inns like Steidl's and the Goldener Hirsch appeal to me most, not just because they're cheap, but because they are busy (a single diner or couple may be
put with you if there are empty seats at your table),
cheerful, and casual. Everybody knows the food is good,
and everybody wants you to enjoy it. But if there's time,
in addition to those mentioned, a hungry traveler should
seek out Am Franziskanerplatz, Auersperg-Palais, Kerzen-
stüberl, Stadtkrug, Wegenstein, Wiener-Rathauskeller,
and Zur Linde, which the Viennese mention with pride,
along with their own favorites among the Hungarian,
Italian, and other foreign restaurants. There are also the
wine taverns like Augustinerkeller, Alter Hofkeller, and
the lower vault of the Urbanikeller, particularly good
late at night.

Just about the cheapest place to eat in town, and one
of the best, is the restaurant attached to the cooking school
operated by the scion of one of Vienna's most famous
chef families, Kofranek. It's hard to find, and worth the
effort. An incomplete address to keep it from getting too
crowded. You sit at banquet tables with knowing Viennese and poor students, a wooden service plate before
you, and eat whatever specialty the student cooks have
prepared under Kofranek's direction. The bread is freshly

baked, the beer is light or dark, the wine is open, and the price for all, including coffee and dessert, is less than two dollars.

Like any love, Vienna doesn't fulfill all one's romantic expectations. It isn't as gay as it was supposed to be in the days of Franz Joseph, but it probably wasn't that carefree even in the days of the monarchy. There are balls and dinners and dances during the winter, and pre-Lenten *Fasching* can become pretty cheery, but Vienna is surely as solidly bourgeois these days as it was in Freud's time there. Vienna wants to be the congress city of Europe, the Continental word for conventions, and there are lots of new hotels a-building, several adequately naked night clubs, and a couple of *avant-garde* theaters that can be pretty biting if you know the Austrian argot. But most people find it a quiet city, with the natives quite conscious that the satellite countries are all along the eastern border. Vienna, incidentally is a good point of departure for those heading for Prague or Bucharest, Budapest or Belgrade.

If you bring your own gaiety along, though, there are plenty of people to share it in the ancient capital of the Habsburgs. Many of the buildings are still painted bright monarchy yellow, the chandeliers still glitter, long mirrors still reflect the white and gilt of the curling baroque, and golden epaulets and braid gleam on the uniforms of porters and captains as a just and proper reminder of military pomp now, one hopes, happily past.

Vienna is a fine jumping-off place from which to explore the rest of Austria. It's only a day to Retz, in the north, whose town square is built over a maze of wine cellars, and where the base of the city tower, the Stadtturm, has been turned into a wine tavern. The surrounding vineyards produce light, fresh whites from the Grüner Veltliner, and if those from Retz aren't the best, then try those from the nearby town of Hangsdorf, where the cooperative is particularly proud of its production. So are the other nearby towns, and each holds spring wine tastings in large barnlike structures where hundreds gather to praise one another's wines. These local *Tasteprobes* are not to be missed, and the *Wurst* and grilled chickens eaten in the fingers are just right with the fresh and glinting wines.

One of the wine towns is Langelois, and north of it is Altenburg, near Horn, the great classic of high *Barock*. Nobody can go to Austria, or be there long, without being touched by the exuberance of the seventeenth-century architectural confectionery—wedding cakes turned inside out—and the swirls of the molded forms echo the sounds of Haydn and Mozart, Beethoven and Brahms, Schubert and Strauss. There's also the dark and heavy sound of Gluck and Bruckner, Mahler and Wolf, to balance the lightness of the Viennese waltzes, so it's no wonder that heavy dark bread and young white wine is such a natural combination, in Vienna or out.

Up the Danube from Vienna is the Wachau, that stretch of river between Melk and Krems bounded by wooded and vine-covered hills, that is considered the loveliest part of the Danube, beautiful as the Mosel. Many of the towns go back a thousand years, for the Wachau is the western entrance to the Hungarian plain, and the ruins of medieval castles still guard the heights. Hikers and canoeists camp where armies bivouacked, and the place where Richard the Lionhearted was held for ransom, the convent in Duernstein, is now an inn, where trout is served bearing a tiny ticket that shows its weight and price. There's no better place to tast the wines of Krems and Loiben and Duernstein, unless it's in the Grill Homar in Krems itself, or the Strandcafe in Spitz. The Muscat-Ottonel and Veltliner are the typical grapes, although the Rhineland varieties such as the Riesling, the Gewürztraminer, and the Sylvaner also produce good wines, as does the Müller-Thurgau, generally considered to be a cross between the Riesling and Sylvaner. Many of the wines go to market under vineyard names, adding to the confusion, so the growers have taken to promoting brand names for their various grades and types, to simplify matters. Some drinkers feel this only compounds it.

In any case, the Wachauers are considered to be the best wines of Austria, and the terraces and courts of the inn of Richard Löwenherz are perfect for drinking them. The river races below, the leafy shade rustles above, and the world is beautiful.

The leading winemaker of the Wachau is Lenz Moser, a stubborn and persevering revolutionary who has fought bitterly for twenty years to introduce a new system of vineyard cultivation that permits the use of tractors. The vine rows are planted a dozen feet apart and allowed to grow tall, the fewer vines producing the same amount of wine from more shoots. The system is being tried in every wine region on earth, and the arguments are long and loud, the tradionalists insisting that the quality of the wines, particularly from the greatest vineyards, is apt to suffer. There's no question that the system works fine in many vineyard areas, and thousands of visitors come to the Wachau each year to listen to Moser and his sons extol the virtues of the new method and inspect the vineyards for themselves.

The most famous wines of Austria come from south of Vienna, from Klosterneuberg and Gumpoldskirchen, and here, too, the countryside is full of inns sporting the wreath that indicates local wine is being sold. As in the Wachau, trout from local streams is a regional specialty, along with grouse and pheasant in season, and as in Vienna the restaurants feature dishes of venison and boar one day a week, for the Austrian loves the full taste of game with the flowery white wines.

Not so far south of Vienna is the province of Burgenland with its orchards and truck gardens and the great, shallow lake called Neusiedlersee, which forms part of the border with Yugoslavia. Eisenstadt is the main town of the province; Haydn is buried here, and there is a palace and park still belonging to the Esterhazy family. The town has a great beehive of a church on a rise in the main square, which has a spiraling tunnel lined with grottoes leading up to its tower. The grottoes are full of life-sized wooden figures, brightly painted, depicting stations of the cross. From the tower you can look across the rich farm country and get the feel of the broad, flat stretches of landscape that distinguish the Hungarian plain. The food, too, picks up foreign accents from gypsy and Croat and Turkish ancestry—all kinds of goulash and dishes with peppers and onions, as well as the more simply cooked Austrian dishes. Perhaps nothing is more typical to eat with wines than *Schmalzbrot*, black bread smeared with delicate lard and sprinkled with paprika.

There are hundreds of cooperatives in the Burgenland, where the Austrian cooperative movement got started, and those to do with wine are responsible for introducing modern methods in the vineyards and establishing wineries where the growers bring their grapes for crushing. Some of the best wines come from Rust, but there are vineyards all around the northern end of the great lake, along the shores of which are several experimental stations where new methods and grapes other than the traditional stocks are being tested. The milder climate makes for fuller, heavier wines than those from the districts nearer Vienna, more suited to the heartier local food. In some years, it is possible to make wine from late-picked grapes, sweet and full, pleasant to drink on special occasions, by themselves or with pastry.

But the sweet wines, and the reds imported from Yugoslavia and Hungary and Italy, are most popular in western Austria, in the Tyrol and the other mountain districts, where winters are long and the food is rich, sustaining, and full of taste. Game and stews, thick soups like *Schwäbische Brot*, hearty cheese dishes, smoky hams and sausages, and pork dishes mark the mountain cuisine in the ski country, and give distinction to the restaurants in Salzburg and Innsbruck and the other resort cities. Plenty of light white wine is drunk, but this is beer country, and the food reflects that of Switzerland and Germany, rather than that of Vienna and Lower Austria. It's still Austrian, and all the specialties are there, and the pastries, but you see a lot more doughnuts and pancakes. After all, there's no place like Vienna, which is a place to fall in love with.

SWITZERLAND

GASTRONOMY. Surrounded by alps, but in constant touch with their Italian, French, German, and Austrian neighbors, the Swiss have adapted the best of all four cuisines, and have added to this their own mountain cooking, which depends heavily on cheese, baked goods, veal, ham, lake fish, and white wine, and seems to vary from alp to alp. Soups are exceptional in Switzerland, as is chocolate, perhaps because of the long, cold, snowy winters, and there's a different sausage with each change of scenery. The distillate of Williams pear called *poire* is unique, as is the absinthe, which was invented in Switzerland and which is illegal but readily available.

BREAKFAST. The Continental breakfast of bread, rolls, and jam, with coffee and milk, is universal, but cheese and ham, eggs, and the other adornments of the English breakfast are available in the hotels. Chocolate, tea, and bouillon are common.

LUNCH & DINNER. Lunch may be light—an omelet, a broiled fish, a stew, or minced veal dish—but dinner usually consists of at least three courses, with wine, beginning with soup and fish, including meat or fowl, salad and dessert, with coffee and brandy, kirsch or poire.

STREET FOOD. Cafés, beer halls, snack bars, tearooms, pastry shops, stand-up counters in supermarkets and department stores, pancake sellers, can be found in all the cities. The railway stations have lunch counters and stands as well as restaurants.

Every country has its national caricature, made up of conflicting attitudes and generalities that are partly true or mostly false, depending on whether you are blowing cold or hot at the moment, and the Swiss manifestation couldn't be more exasperating. For the past half-dozen generations, or longer, the Swiss have been running around with their tongues in their cheeks (this accounts for the up-down, slow-quick of "Schwyzerdütsch" that's so incomprehensible you feel you're going to understand it in about five minutes and one more drink), letting strangers believe that all the women are versions of Heidi, or cowgirls in dirndls with forefingers stuck in the corners of their shy smiles, that the men are all ex-cliffhangers just come from a yodeling session. The Swiss occasionally seem to believe this about themselves, until pressed. Then they pretend that they're watchmakers, cheesemakers, hotelkeepers, chefs, bakers, skiers, skaters, chocolate boilers, dried-food packagers, or whatever else they think the stranger might like to hear at the moment.

"We're such a small country," they say, turning their backs on the great mountains, vast lakes, and rich valleys of the most massive scenery in Europe. "We're less than six million, so we're neutral," they say, putting aside the fact that this peaceable approach has bulged the banks with money from all over the globe, the first flow

of which came from Swiss mercenaries that were the
backbone of every European army for centuries. "We
work too hard," they say, avoiding momentarily the
fact that they always seem to have time for another
drink; that they display vast knowledge of food and
wine indicating endless hours spent in consumption, at
the same time sporting trim figures that point to many
sunny days spent in healthful outdoor activity. The most
irritating thing about the Swiss is their bland assumption
that the stranger is gullible enough to swallow such
guff, and the most astounding thing is that we do. This
pretense of a national inferiority complex has proved
to be Switzerland's greatest developed resource, and has
become its most important export, in Europe at least,
where every country seems to have adopted it for themselves as a way to get ahead in the world and mulct lucre
from neighbors and passing tourists.

The Swiss would have you believe that their national
diet is meager, consisting almost entirely of diced (not
minced) veal called *geschnetzeltes Kalbfleisch;* a soup of
stock thickened with browned flour called *geröstete
Mehlsuppe;* thinly sliced or riced boiled potatoes sautéed
until crusty and called *Rösti;* a kind of tiny simmered
egg noodle or dumpling called *Spätzli* or *Knöpfli;* and
great slabs of cheese, called *Gruyère* or *Emmenthaler.*
Toss in a *fondu* made with kirsch and white wine; add
Raclette, which consists of slowly melting half a wheel
of cheese, preferably before a wood fire, then devouring
the melted scrapings with forkfuls of boiled potatoes;
include a few cookies and you've just about had it.

Not so. Every valley and town has versions of these,
slightly different and delicious, its own kind of smoked

or air-dried ham or sausage, several cheese and potato dishes cooked either separately or together, its own individual stew or *pot au feu*, and its own special breads, tarts or flans (called *Wähen* and filled with fruits, mashed vegetables, cheese mixtures or custards), cakes, pancakes of all sorts, and fritters.

Just about anything is dipped in a batter and fried in Switzerland: sage leaves in Zurich; bunches of cherries, or apples, peaches or pears, just about everywhere; and in Grisons there's *gonterser Bock*, which is a hard-boiled egg dipped successively in batter until it's as big as a baseball; not to mention fish fritters, cheese fritters, zucchini and eggplant fritters, and just plain fritters. When they're sprinkled with sugar, they're served as dessert.

Every lake and stream has its fish, the most famous of which is the landlocked salmon of Berne, *omble chevalier*, which used to be presented to startled visiting dignitaries the Bernese really wanted to honor. The German-speaking north and east borrow lavishly from the German and Austrian cuisine, the French-speaking west adapts anything French that's desirable, and the Italian-speaking south makes free with all things Italian. With just, due and self-effacing modesty, of course, which is why so many Swiss words are diminutives, to minimize the cheery brigandry. When all these dishes get into the Alps they take on an individual character of their own, and then move out again to the foothills to form a special cuisine that is no longer national, but is best called mountain cookery. It's Swiss, though, the Swiss being great ones for taking things in, fiddling around, then sending them out again, chocolate from the East, for example, or a few cents' worth of imported steel that is converted into springs and precision parts worth thousands. Not to mention the cuisine of all nations.

About the worst thing you can blame on the Swiss is International Cuisine. Of course, they naturally did a good job of it, but that's scarcely an excuse. When they decided to get out of the soldier-supplying business at the turn of the eighteenth century, they cast about for some other way to part royalty from their treasure. Their eyes lit upon the craggy, snowy alps and the rocky shores of lakes, nice to look at, but not productive. It's probably not true that they pitted the English against the Germans to see which could climb the highest. But it was about this time that foreigners with more nerve than sense took up the sport of mountain climbing, aided always by careful, sure-footed Swiss guides who pointed out the most dangerous places to climb. They observed the skis of the Norwegians and the skates of the Dutch, and put them at the disposal of tourists they enticed to flounder on the snow and ice. They put up inns and hotels wherever there was even a passable view so that the dwindling aristocracy and the burgeoning well-to-do could rub shoulders and observe the views together. And they set up schools to train the citizenry in how to feed and bed them so that visitors scarcely realized they were parting with all that money.

If, today, it seems that every palace hotel and three-star restaurant is run by a Swiss, it's because they so early developed a standard of service and sustenance. The cooking schools train chefs in French cookery, not just because it's the best in the world, but because things

French are still the fashion in the *haut monde*, members of which have to be ready spenders to stay in good standing. All the dishes are adapted a little; and while all the chefs learn the same recipes, each has his own improvements, so a certain similarity creeps into menus in a certain type of hotel, wherever it happens to be. And the schools aren't above inventing dishes when things get dull. The method of cooking bits of meat in a bubbling pot of oil right at the table, for instance, is called *fondue bourguignonne*, and is from an old Turkish recipe resurrected at one of the hotel schools in Lausanne. The name is French, of course, the Swiss *hôteliers* knowing exactly what they're doing.

If you can keep out of the resort hotels, however, you can avoid all this elegant, monotonous excellence, which is only occasionally a delight—when you want a rest, for instance, or when you're on a honeymoon. There's mountain cookery in all the small inns. But before you desert the cities, try the perch or the variety of land-locked salmon called *ombre chevalier* in Geneva or Lausanne; *fondue* with butter, cream, and croutons, or the Geneva tart of white wine, cinnamon, and sugar called *sèche au vin*.

The *matafan* of Fribourg which is a batter lightened with whipped whites that's poured over bread sopped in hot milk, and baked. Don't forget *gâteau fribourgeoise*, which is an almond mixture under a pastry lattice, made spicy with candied lemon rind.

The *Berner Platte* is available anywhere—sauerkraut with ham, bacon, pork bits, and the famous Bernese tongue sausage. There's *Basler Läckerli*, which are molded nut spice cookies, the thin wine and kirsch pancakes that are fried in deep fat, then sugared, and the *Krapfen*, which are a sort of dessert ravioli fried to gold and filled with walnuts and stewed pears.

In Zurich are the tiny bits of liver wrapped in sage, stuck on little wooden skewers and sautéed in butter; the hotpot of pork and cabbage; the square, thick carnival pancakes, and *Eieröhrli*, also eaten at carnival, extra thin pancakes fried to a crisp in butter, then sprinkled with sugar. While there, don't miss the ancient bakery, Conditorei Schober, in a house that dates from the middle of the fourteenth century, where chocolates shaped in antique forms are laid out on velvet, and the old cookie molds are brought out every Christmas for making batches of the whitish *Anismodel*. In all the shops there are *Maikafer*, chocolate beetles with almond wings, and the bakeries have *Bürli*, fat, well-browned rolls baked in quartets, tough and chewy peasant bread that's just right with hot sausages.

The sausages. There's the mild veal *Bratwurst*, which has a special shape and taste in the Vaud, and is called *Waadtländer Bratwurst* in the German-speaking parts. But pride of place goes to the *Beinwurst* from Grisons, the queen of sausages according to the Swiss, just the thing after a hard hike in the mountains. Watch out, it contains bits of bone. The wine country has its own sausages, among them those with leeks, cabbage, or liver. All this will give you some idea of what the Swiss can do to food.

If you can't wait to get out of the cities, go to Zug. It's only half an hour from Zurich and it's the kirsch capital of the world. It's also the home city of companies from forty-seven different countries, including over a hundred from the United States, the Swiss having noted the unfriendly tax laws of other lands, then made their own conveniently hospitable. It's scarcely a main street long, but there's the Restaurant Aklin next to the town tower, the Rathskeller just around the corner, where you knock for beer by drumming the base of your glass on the table, each rattle of knocks counted by the waitress so she'll know how many seidels to bring. On certain nights it's full of students, the young ones called foxes, who fetch and carry for the upperclassmen and graduates, who are called the old boys. It's the Swiss way of providing extra help when things get rushed, and of implicitly showing the foxes the advantages of higher education and the need for passing exams. Right down the street is the firm of Etter & Fils, whose senior partner is the president of the kirsch producer's association.

Strangers think kirsch is something to pour on orange slices or lace into a *fondue*, if they know about it at all, but that all changes after a few hours in Zug. A Bavarian may have beer for breakfast, but a Zug breakfast is kirsch and coffee, which tastes equally good in midmorning. Lunch may start with Weissflog, which is a chilled and lightly alcoholic bitters, but in Zug it's improved with kirsch. Or there's vermouth-kirsch, two parts of sweet vermouth to one of kirsch, well chilled. A meal ends with that best of Swiss pastries, *Kirschtorte*, a crusty, creamy wedge of sugary tart, followed by kirsch and coffee, followed by beer and small glasses of chilled kirsch, because kirsch makes you thirsty. Zugers say hot bouillon with kirsch is a fine way to start the day and best for the end of an evening, too.

There are some three hundred varieties of cherries, but

only a half-dozen make fine kirsch. The white blossoms make foamy mounds in the spring green fields and meadows. The trees aren't planted in rows, as in American orchards, and in July you can see groups of people moving from tree to tree wherever the old tradition of the cherry auction still prevails. Kirsch-makers buy treefuls of cherries. A good tree often bears a thousand pounds of fruit, and some distillers seek the fruit of a thousand trees. There are said to be a million and a half cherry trees in Switzerland, and until the first decade of the eighteenth century the law stated that the cherries belonged to the birds and the people who wanted them.

The cherries come to the distillers in barrels, where they are allowed to ferment for a month, after which they are distilled in small pot stills, usually twice distilled for the best qualities, to an alcoholic percentage between 57 and 60, between 115 and 120 proof. A hundred liters of cherry mash produces about a liter of kirsch, not much more than a quart, and if you try to get more, quality suffers.

Kirsch is not aged in wood, but is stored in demijohns in a loft above the stillhouse, where the heat of summer and chill of winter help develop the bouquet and taste of the kirsch. The demijohns, called bon-bons, are loosely stoppered so that the air can get at the clear white liquid. In the neck of each is a slip of paper containing the year of distilling, the proof, and various code numbers that show the source of the cherries and other pertinent data, quality depending on the excellence of the cherries and the art of the distilling. The bon-bons stay in the lofts for five years while the kirsch mellows. It's something to see, a loft floor covered with perhaps a thousand jugs, all full of kirsch. Here and there are bon-bons of distillations made twenty or thirty years ago and a whiff or taste can bring back a childhood spring.

The people of Zug are also experts on beer, which they consider a fine chaser for good old kirsch. One list of favorites includes the Eichof beer of Lucerne, Warteck from Basel, Löwenbräu from Zurich, Cardinal from Fribourg, and Feldschlossli or Hopfer-Perle from Basel. An excellent light lunch in warm weather is cold ham, preferably from Grisons, little red radishes with butter, and a big beer, followed by a Brissago, which is a strong and skinny black cigar, lit by setting it across the top of a glass and holding a match to the tip. They come from the town of the same name in Italian Switzerland, and are almost as strong as Toscanellis, which are short and black and smoked after dinner, with kirsch and coffee.

The local inhabitants are also fond of white wines, which they have with local fish, the best of which is the *Zugerrötel,* and Zugers tell you it should swim three times, first in water, then in butter, then in white wine. Perhaps because the saying is not original, the locals insist on poaching another favorite, *Felchen,* which is called *féra* in the French parts of the country, in a veal stock, although perch and trout are often simmered in wine. You shouldn't leave town without trying the potato cake, which is made by covering a layer of mashed potatoes with a mixture of beaten eggs, cream, and grated Gruyère, then baking it for half an hour. In the neighboring canton of Schwyz, which is the first and oldest and the home of William Tell and the one from which the country takes its name, the local potato cake is called *Ofentürli,* and is made by working some flour into a couple of pounds of mashed potatoes, adding lots of butter, and baking in a hot oven until well browned.

Schwyz is also famous for kirsch, the largest producer being Dettling of Brunnen. The head of the firm takes pleasure in recommending the Dettlong, a drink invented by American GIs on leave after the war, made by adding kirsch to a tall glass of tonic water. The best restaurant in Brunnen is Schmid's, and in the country towns around are others: Ried's in Muotatal is primitive but noted for its local trouts; Schwert's in Gersau is famous for its fish from the lake of Lucerne; the Seehotel and the Zugersee in Walchwil are both distinguished for their French cooking in the Swiss style; and in the town of Schwyz itself is the Hotel Wysses Rossli, which has been in the same family for seven generations and has been famous all that time for trout and veal dishes. It's not the original of the White Horse Inn, there being hundreds of White Horse Inns all over the alps, in and out of Switzerland.

This heart of the cherry country is typically Swiss, if any part of such a varied land can be so called, and if you seek a change from kirsch there's always Williams to enchant you. The distillate of this particular pear variety is exceptional and is discovered with cries of wild delight by any tourist who stays around for longer than two days. He's sure to leave lugging as many bottles as is allowed. The most startling have full-grown pears inside. This Swiss version of the ship-in-a-bottle puzzle is done by slipping the bottle over the pear when it is first formed, so that the pear grows inside the bottle—as big as possible, hope the Swiss, for the larger the pear the less of expensive poire they have to put inside. Like kirsch, Williams is aged in crocks, to keep it colorless, and is served chilled.

The most famous drink in Switzerland is absinthe. Its base is wormwood, it is supposed to be habit-forming, it is potent, it tastes of licorice, it is bluish green in color, turning opalescent when mixed with water, and it is illegal almost everywhere in the world, particularly in Switzerland, where it was invented about a century ago by a French expatriate. It is also delicious, so the Swiss have only forbidden its sale, which means it is available anywhere. Not under the name of absinthe, though, and you ought to have some acquaintance with the proprietor of the place where you order it, meaning that you've ordered a drink or two or said you plan to stick around for dinner. After establishing a rapprochement, you boldly ask for *une bleu* or *une verte* in Neuchâtel, *une blanche* in Fribourg, or perhaps *une ficelle* or *du lait* elsewhere. All the names refer to the color, before or after water is added, except "the string" which seems to refer to that band tightening slowly around your brow during an absinthe hangover. Any one of the names will do, and all of them are French because it's most readily available in French Switzerland. It tastes like its anise imitators, and unscrupulous proprietors may foist on you the legal substitutes, but you should be able to tell the difference after three or so.

The most famous Swiss wines come from Neuchâtel, light, fresh, whites made from the Chasselas grape. They are bottled promptly after the vintage, and go through a slight second fermentation in the bottle, consequently they show a slight sparkle in the glass. This is called *spritzig* in German, *pétillant* in French, and *frizzante* in Italian, so it is natural that the winemakers of Neuchâtel refer to the slight beading and the bubbles on the surface of the glass as *l'étoile*. The star doesn't hurt the wine at all, looks pretty, in fact, and to make it show best, the bottle is held high above the glass as it is poured. This causes a ring of big bubbles to form around the glass, called the *cordon*, and this is supposed to add to the pleasing appearance.

Neuchâtel boasts a wine museum, the Château de Bondine, where you can order the local sausage and local wines for lunch, and right down the road is a little place where you can get snails, the escargots d'Areuse, which the Swiss insist are the best in the world. There's also a fine restaurant in the Neuchâtel station, where you can get all the local specialties, including a dish of lettuce, sausage, and bacon that is on a par with the sausage-stuffed cabbage that's a specialty of Zug. The railroad restaurants in the Swiss stations are famous, and they vie with one another to get the seasonal specialties first, the Cavaillon asparagus, for instance, or the mountain cheeses. Here you can also get the original *fondue*, which is said to have been invented in nearby Gruyère by a monk during Lent, when the cheese, as well as milk and eggs, were forbidden. When melted, the monk reasoned, it was no longer cheese, and therefore permitted.

Gruyère is one of the greatest of all cheeses, and scarce, much smaller than the Emmenthaler, and more delicate in flavor. Nobody should miss visiting a cheese factory while in Switzerland, and there are hundreds. Emmenthaler sent to the United States is milder than that eaten in Switzerland, incidentally, so it shouldn't be missed while you're there. It's probably not possible, in any case.

A much bigger wine district is the Vaud, whose vineyards are planted along the banks of Lake Geneva, the section called La Côte to the west of Lausanne with Lavaux to the east, and the Chablais, a southern extension along the banks of the Rhône, where it enters Lake Geneva. Dézaley and St.-Saphorin are the best known Lavaux townships, Yvorne and Aigle the ones in Chablais, perhaps Fèchy and Luins the ones of La Côte, although there are many others in each section. In all, the Vaud produces some 35 million gallons in a normal year, mostly Chasselas, Neuchâtel produces 5 million, but the best wines of all come from further up the Rhône, the Valais, which produces more than both together.

The best wines of the Valais come from around the town of Sion, and in the stretch extending up to Sierre, with a few interesting whites coming from still further upstream, in the township of Visp, which boasts the highest vineyards in Europe.

The Valais is a lovely long valley so protected by mountains that palm trees grow, as well as the rosy blooming tamarisse, which was imported from Egypt centuries ago. The largest producer is the cooperative, Provins, which produces not only the Fendant, the most popular of the Valais wines, made from the Chasselas, but several specialties, including Johannisberg, which is made from the German Sylvaner grape, Hermitage, Malvoisie, Arvine, Amigne, and Muscat. Red wine made from Burgundy's Pinot, primarily, is sold as Dôle de Sion, and there is Vin du Glacier, a hard white wine stored for years in the high mountain villages. Other whites come from vineyards around Geneva, and some good reds from the Merlot grape come from the Italian-speaking Ticino.

All of them taste wonderful near the place of origin, and the white wines ship well. There's nothing quite like drinking Fendant, though, in the old inn in Sierre, a plate of air-dried Grisons ham before you, a plate of tiny new potatoes steaming in a napkin, the low-beamed room filled with the spicy, gingerbread-y smell of Gruyère melting before the fire, waiting for the pretty girl to serve you the first scrapings from the wheel. Raclette is a Valais specialty, and it tastes best here.

ITALY

GASTRONOMY. Bounded by the fruits of the sea, rich with olive oil and tomatoes in the south, vibrant with rosemary, oregano, and basil in the north, blessed with a tradition of cuisine that goes back before the Romans, Italy is a land of regional specialties, each great city a gastronomic center borrowing from the countryside and vitalized with ancient adaptations from the Orient and eastern Mediterranean. Noodles came from China with Marco Polo, to be glorified into the vast array of *pastas* that form a course on every Italian menu, along with the Italian version of the Chinese stir-fry, the quick-cooking of thin slices of veal or beef pounded thinner, juices sealed in with a high, hot flame. Suckling pig and baby veal, game and wildfowl, the earliest and smallest of vegetables, rich mixtures of rice, polenta and other grains, hard and soft cheeses, bread sticks, pizzas and countless loaves are syncopated into meals, grand or homely, that are matched to the season and the moment by the genius of good Italian cooks.

BREAKFAST. Coffee with milk and bread with marmalade and other jams, often with seasonal fruits. English and American breakfasts in the large hotels.

LUNCH. Generally in the simpler type of restaurant called a *trattoria;* perhaps only a *minestra,* which is pasta with a sauce or in broth, a rich soup with vegetables like minestrone, or a saffron rich dish, perhaps followed by a fish or meat stew. Often enough, lunch is bread, wine, cheese and sausages like bologna or salami, or a vast salad, or something grilled in a *rosticceria,* pizza in a *pizzeria,* or delicatessen in a *birreria.*

DINNER. A *ristorante* or old style *hosteria* or *taverna* will serve several courses with wine, beginning with antipasto, followed by soup or pasta, then fish or sea food, chicken or meat, salad and dessert.

STREET FOOD. Carts and barrows sell ice cream, taffy, sausages, and what-have-you, the cafés and *pasticcerie* feature pastry and drinks and delicatessen, the *gelateria* serves fine ice cream, and *sale da tè,* snack bars and counter places, serve the usual tea, sandwiches, and ready-to-eat foods.

Italian chefs are the most imaginative in Europe, they are the boldest, and the food is the most varied and the most exciting. With this often-true generality out of the way, waving good-bye to our outraged French friends in that symbolic gesture of all guidebooks since Exodus, let us turn south to the bountiful boot.

From France, travelers arrive on the Italian Riviera to find Genoa and its glorious *il pesto* sauce of mashed basil, pine nuts, salty Sardo cheese, garlic, and olive oil, best on shoestring noodles called *trenette,* or whatever else the chef thinks might be good with it, except perhaps for ravioli, which is a Genoese invention. There's also *gnocchi*, a sort of dumpling, *zuppa di pesce*, which is a fish stew like bouillabaisse and which is different and usually delicious all along the Mediterranean and Atlantic coast regardless of name and country. *Cappon magro*, queen of salads, is diced vegetables on a crusty base, topped with fish and sea food. The red wines are Dolceacqua and Rossesse, the whites, Coronata and Cinque Terre, the last grown in coastal vineyards so steep the grapes are lowered into boats and sailed away to the presshouses.

If you are coming from Austria, you'll get to Venice, with its cafés and the bands in St. Mark's square, Harry's Bar, where the Martinis, at least, are still cheap, and endless restaurants and snack stands in the warren of streets. You can find *fritto misto*, a mixed fish fry; *risi e bisi*, rice and peas with bacon; *risi e peoci*, another *risotto* but with local clams; *fegato alla veneziana*, the original calves' liver and onions, and fish of all sorts and sizes. The white Soave and red Valpolicella are popular in Venice, and the pink *rosato*, Lagarino.

There are even more fish in Trieste, which once was the capital of that part of the Dalmatian coast which is now Yugoslavia, and they are prepared better than anywhere else in Italy—until, of course, you stop in another coastal town, where they will be glorious, too. Trieste is two towns, one around the harbor and the other on the surrounding hills, and in both of them the favorite drink is brandy by Stock, the immense Italian firm that sells more brandy than any other firm. There are also a flock of Austrian dishes, one being *iota triestina*, spare ribs and pig's feet with beans and sauerkraut. There's also Hungarian *gulyás*, or goulash. All are good with wines made from German grapes, called here Termeno, the also-white Terlano, Verdiso, and Prosecco. Reds include Caldaro, Santa Maddalena, Marzemino, and Teroldego.

Arriving from Switzerland in the lake country of Lombardy and the shores of Como, Maggiore, or Garda, you will eventually reach Milan, the richest city of Italy, blessed with the exuberant and lavish La Scala, the flamboyant center of the world of opera. *Minestrone* was invented here, it's served hot or cold, and the breaded veal cutlet, *costoletta alla milanese*, tender and juicy inside, crisp and golden outside, always served with lemon, as are most fried and broiled meats. *Risotto milanese* is the classic, saffron rice cooked in white wine and chicken stock with marrow, and *osso bucco*, braised veal shanks, both served with the illustrious *gremolada sauce*, of rosemary, sage, garlic, white wine, and lemon peel. The red wines are from the Valtellina and are called Sassella and Grumella, Inferno and Valgella. There's also a white. Other whites are the southern Frecciarossa, and the Lugana, from the shores of Lake Garda, which also produce light reds and *rosatos* called Valtanesi, Chiaretto, and Moniga.

Now that a tunnel is under Mont Blanc, you can arrive directly in the Piedmont, which produces the best wines of Italy. The finest are from the Nebbiolo grape—Barolo, Barbaresco, Gattinara, and Carema—but wines from such grapes as Grignolino, Barbera, and Freisa are also good. These wines are called *vini generosi*, full and big in comparison to the ordinary wines so often found, and called *vini di pasto*. Whites from the district are mostly sweet and made from dried (*passito*) grapes, the best being Caluso or Moscato d'Asti. The Muscat also produces a sweet sparkling wine in Asti, called Asti Spumante, naturally enough, but drier versions from Burgundy's Pinot Chardonnay are now preferred. The whites, and some of the reds, are sometimes allowed to be *frizzante* or *amabile*—slighty sparkling. You can avoid it by ordering *asciutto,* meaning dry. The only good dry white is Cortese.

The food of Piedmont is crowned by its white truffles, *tartufi*, features of most Piedmont dishes, including the magnificent wild fowl and game. The classic sauce of the region is hot *bagna cauda*, a blend of anchovies, truffles, and garlic with oil and butter, into which vegetables and other bits are dipped. The classic dish is *il bollito,* a boiled dinner that varies from place to place, and is magnificent. The *fonduta* is a more delicate version of the Swiss *fondue,* with truffles. Turin, the wine capital of the region, is home to most of the big wine and vermouth firms of the area, most of whom delight in welcoming visitors.

Bologna, the gastronomic capital of Italy, lies in Emilia, just below the border provinces. Everybody delights in telling you there's no baloney in Bologna, but *mortadella*, instead, the large red and white sausages that date back to the Middle Ages. All kinds of rich *pasta* dishes and pork dishes come from Bologna, and it's no city to go if weight's a problem, or if you're looking for scenery, because most of it is flat, thus fertile. Old towns are strung along the Via Emilia, all famous for food, but most tourists ignore it, heading down the coast for Pisa, or over the hills to Florence, and glorious Tuscany. The

local reds include Lambrusco and Sangiovese, the white
is Albana.

Chianti comes from the vineyards in the hills near
Florence and tastes best with the local specialties, a list
easily a kilometer long that includes: *uccelletti*, larks and
small birds flavored with laurel and roasted on a spit;
uccelletti scappati, which are veal birds; a *fritto misto*
sautéed in oil (butter is used in Milan) that includes lamb,
brains, sweetbreads, chicken livers, and vegetables, all
breaded; the famous *bistecca alla fiorentina* is a small
steak from a young steer brushed with olive oil and
quickly broiled; *tortino carciofi* is a baked omelet with
artichokes. The list goes on and on. Tuscany is a wonderful place to eat, and there's always fruity Chianti to
drink, the best of which comes in regular wine bottles,
not the straw-covered fiaschi.

Books have been written about eating in Rome, the
joys of Frascati and the other wines from the Roman hills,
the *castelli Romani*, which include Albano and Velletri,
Marino and Ariccia, Genzano and Rocca di Papa. From
over on the Adriatic come the light red Rosso Piceno, the
white Verdicchio and Orvieto, and that famous but ordinary wine of Montefiascone, Est! Est!! Est!!! Dishes not
to miss are *saltimbocca*, which is thin veal slices sautéed
with prosciutto ham and sage; *fettuccine alla romana*, thin
noodles swirled with butter and Parmesan cheese, and the
version called *maestose fettuccine al triplo burro*, or the
kind with four cheeses, *quattro formaggi*; *abbacchio* is
suckling pig that rivals the Spanish version; *carciofi alla
romana* are tiny artichokes simmered in olive oil and white
wine.

You can be your own guide, but the Italians swear by
the *Vademecum*, published by the Italian Touring Club
each year, rating restaurants and listing specialties all over
Italy, like Michelin. Many travelers insist, though, that
the Michelin for Italy is a still better guide.

Naples is the home of the pizza, and only a boat ride
away are Capri and Ischia, famous for white wines.
There's Sardinia in the sea to the west, a marvelous combination of France and Italy because it's so near Corsica,
and there is rugged Sicily to the south, famous for Marsala,
which was invented by an Englishman, a full sweet wine
meant to compete with Spanish sherry on the English
markets. The wine that's most like sherry, but with its
own distinctive dryness, is Vernaccia, produced on Sardinia. There's also the sweet Malvasia from the islands of
Lipari and the district of Vulture.

All over Italy, the wines vary, depending on who makes
it and how. A Barolo can be glorious, or a Chianti, or
they can be ordinary. Generally, the full reds of the Piedmont and Lombardy are consistently the best, although
Valpolicella from the eastern shores of Lake Garda and
the lighter Bardolino are well-made, as are the best
Chiantis. The best white is probably Soave, from the
region near Verona. But the thing to drink is the local
wine, taking your chances on the taste of the innkeeper;
if the food is good, the wine will be, too.

The simple things of Italian kitchens are what one re-
members most, ripe melons served with a sliver of prosciutto, for instance, the *grissini* of Turin, bread sticks so
thin and crisp and tasty you can't stop eating them, the
cheeses—Bel Paese, Stracchino, and the noble Gorgon-
zola from Lombardy, the balls of mozzarella from Naples,

ricotta, cacciocavallo, fior d'Alpi. The sausages are as varied as the cheeses, as the *paste*, as the *risotti* of the north. A lot of the cooking is fast, a method perhaps coming from the Chinese, like the *piccata*, steak pounded thin and cooked on a greased griddle, or the way greens are done, quickly stirred in a little sizzling fat.

The Italians like to eat in different kinds of places, on the streets, in the cafés, in the little restaurants called *trattorie*, in grills called *rosticerrie*, and snack bars are becoming popular, too. But best of all, he likes a hearty lunch and dinner, starting with an *antipasto*, a platter that includes just about anything cold, but mostly raw vegetables and sliced sausages, olives, and various pickled dishes, certainly some anchovies or sardines or tuna. This will be followed by *minestre*, a small serving of a *pasta* or a soup, large quantities of which might become almost a main course at a simple lunch, and would certainly be considered a meal by Americans. This is followed by a *ragù*, or stew, some boiled or broiled fish, fowl in some way, or a meat dish. Generally there's a salad or vegetable with the main course. And then comes cheese and fruit, or dessert, and coffee. It's hearty eating. But just as often, an Italian will settle for a piece of bread and cheese for lunch, and a piece of fruit. More and more, all over Europe, eating is becoming a matter of one main meal a day, lunch or dinner.

Italian cooking is a surprise to most Americans at first, for Italian restaurants in the United States have made Sicilian and Neapolitan cooking synonymous with Italian, the ankle, the foot, and the ball representing the whole boot. That's changing, now, of course, and all to the good. But Italy is still a revelation, full of moments.

There's the time, for instance, when you suddenly realize that freshly made *pasta* is nothing at all like the dried ribbons we use all the time, and that just plain spaghetti with butter sauce can be a dish for the gods of gastronomy. Then there's the time when you realize the very taste of the *pasta* changes with its shape, as well as with the sauces put on it.

Or there's the first time you have a seemingly simple dish like the *fonduta* variation which is small balls of cheese rolled in crumbs then deep fried, and served with crisp fried sprigs of parsley. There's veal with tuna sauce, *vitello tonnato*, a pale sauce of cream and mashed tuna with capers, poured over slices of cold veal, on a bed of rice; and there's *le vere lasagne verdi al forno alla bolognese*, one of the great dishes of Italian cuisine, green noodles with a meat sauce and a nutmeg cream sauce, sprinkled with Parmesan and finished in the oven. There's even *cannelloni*, a modern dish but good, sometimes, patterned after quenelles, but usually delicate noodle dough filled with a forcemeat and served with a sauce. Every restaurant has *cannelloni;* wait until you taste a good one.

That's the point about traveling in Italy, in fact. A bad wine, a bad dish? Maybe the cook's wife got mad at him that morning, maybe it's a rainy day, maybe you hit a bad restaurant. Tonight, at dinner, you're sure to hit it lucky. There's always hope for the best in Italy.

IBERIA
Spain & Portugal

GASTRONOMY. The long coast provides a bounty of fish and shellfish, which are simply fried or combined with rice to make rich dishes. Fish stews are common along the coast, and the mountain streams provide trout and crayfish. Olives and almonds from the south, peppers, tomatoes and other garden vegetables, are all combined with poultry or meats to make a vast number of stews, one of the most ancient being *olla podrida*, which varies with the locale. Ham and sausages vary with every province, but perhaps nothing is served in so many ways as eggs, which appear with sauces, in omelets with pimiento and peppers, in various aspics, and fried in various ways. Game and wildfowl are plentiful, and suckling pigs are a spring treat.

BREAKFAST. A kind of cruller and coffee with a glass of anise is a homely breakfast, but bread and rolls with marmalade, and coffee with milk, are most common. The hotels serve English breakfasts. Fruits such as oranges and melons are served in season.

LUNCH & DINNER. Bread, cheese and wine, followed by fruit, and perhaps including ham or sausages, make a frequent lunch. An egg dish or a stew is often served, and a cold soup is on most menus in summer. Dinner is usually served after ten, at least three courses with wine, starting with soup or fish, and including meat or fowl. Sherry is customary before meals, brandy generally follows.

STREET FOOD.   *Tapas*—slivers of ham and cheese—are served in every bar and *bodega*, which is a sort of café. Street hawkers vend almonds and peanuts, shrimp and sausages, oranges and sweet biscuits. Saucers of olives and almonds are available in every café. A few snack bars and lunch counters have appeared in Madrid and Barcelona and Lisbon, but elsewhere the venders still reign. Sandwiches are available in most cafés, pastry and delicatessen in the coffeeshops.

Oil. Everything's cooked in oil, oil, oil, say the whip-through tourists, the same old oil, used over and over again. What's more, they don't eat lunch till three, dinner until ten, or maybe later, you could starve to death. But it's cheap. A depressed country, full of fire and grandeur, fish and saffron rice, great people, but that olive oil!

Which makes it easy, of course, because you can pick restaurants by smell, and there are plenty of good ones around, as a check in the French Michelin will show. But because the poor ones are so obvious, tourists have a tendency to stick to tourist traps with international menus, dull at best, missing small places where the long-cooked stews and the quick, casually cooked fish or egg dishes are better than good. Spain is also a country for roasts, done in open dome ovens over wood fires, and

there's nothing to touch the suckling piglets of spring at
Botín's in Madrid, or just about anywhere else, for that
matter. And there are the tomato, pepper, and garlic
dishes from the Catalan country around Barcelona, tuna
fish, for instance, that have been dubbed Provençale by
the French. To find out how good they can be, drive
up the Rioja valley, not too far from Barcelona, and try
them with the full red wines.

Over on the Atlantic is Basque country, where there
are steamed clams, *almejas,* and chopped crab, *centolla,*
and squid, called *calamares* when they're grown, *chipi-
rones* when they're not, quickly fried, or served in rich
sauces. There are the shrimps and prawns, *camarones* and
gambas, crawfish and lobster, *langostina* and *langosta,*
cooked simply or with rich sauces, and the best place to
have them is in one of the eating clubs, where the men
do their own cooking. Cod and hake, *bacalao* and *mer-
luza,* are prepared in dozens of ways, and in winter baby
eels are fried in a batter and served with slices of chili
pepper, one of the great dishes of Spain.

There's no doubt that the best cooking is home cooking in Spain, and because so much eating is done at home,
restaurants aren't common, except in the cities. Men in
cafés drink wine and beer and nibble *tapas:* almonds, small
olives, slivers of cheese and ham, a handful of small shrimp
bought from a peddler and shucked like peanuts. If it's
in the south, the wine may be a pale dry light Sherry,
a *fino,* but more often it's apt to be a glass of the local
red or white.

Anise is a favorite drink in Spain, the modern version
of absinthe, available dry or sweet, and turning cloudy
when water is added. The dry ones are often drunk

straight, with or in coffee. In the north, the favorite kind is Anís del Mono, but those of Chinchon are generally preferred in Madrid.

Puchero is chickpea stew with chicken, beef, and bacon that's a Madrid specialty, and *cocido* is a similar one. These vary all over the country, as do *paellas*, which are saffron rice dishes including various meats and fish and sea food. What is known as *paella* in the States is really *arroz a la valenciana*, and both rice dishes also vary from province to province, depending on local ingredients. Nothing varies so much as the cold vegetable soup, *gazpacho*, which is sometimes thickened with bread crumbs and sometimes kept as clear as possible; either way, it's wonderful.

The Spanish have a way with eggs, not the least of which is *tortilla española*, one of the many omelets, which is browned on both sides, without folding, being carefully turned out on a plate, then eased back into the pan, uncooked side down. In Rioja, they use ham, the small sausages called *chorizo*, and pimiento to make a distinctive omelet. Great things are also done with poached eggs and coddled eggs, which are served in aspics and various sauces, so that the yolk breaks and runs when pierced by a fork. Eggs are also fried in about an inch of oil so that they crisp.

At all the fairs, particularly the big one in Sevilla, you'll get *buñuelos*, which are rounds of dough tossed into caldrons of fat, then drained and sprinkled with sugar. They are similar to *churros*, which is dough squirted out of a tube and into fat until it is brown, the hot and hollow lengths being sprinkled with sugar. It used to be just the thing to go with breakfast coffee.

The fruits of Spain, not only the Seville oranges and the many kinds of melons, but all orchard and bush fruits, are exceptional, and the rare and special ones like kumquats and pomegranates, custard apples and prickly pears, show the influence of the Moors, and the long connections with Africa. The saffron, pimiento, paprika, and rice are all inheritances from the Moors.

Tourists have discovered Málaga and the Mediterranean islands, but few get to Jerez and Cádiz, just south of Sevilla. Jerez, and its satellite towns of Puerto de Santa Maria and Sanlucar de Barrameda, produce the Spanish sherries from the vineyards in the triangle formed by the three towns. Nobody knows why the fermenting wine works so strangely, some forming a yeast called the *flor* on top of a fermenting cask. When this flower appears, the wine will become a *fino*. Some of these wines will need extra years to mature because it is so full and stout —*gordo* is the Spanish word—and these produce a special type called Amontillado. If no *flor* forms, the type called *oloroso* will be made. And in Sanlucar there's a special type of *fino*, unique because of the salt air, it is said. Called *manzanilla*, it is the driest wine in all the world, perfect by itself, with *tapas*, with shellfish and fish, and hardly known outside the district. Each night there's a fish auction at Sanlucar, and one can sit on a covered balcony raised above the sand, drinking *manzanilla*, eating fish, and watching horse-drawn carts full of ice splash out to the boats for the catch. The fishermen's wives and children sit on the sand, watching the local restaurant owner auction the fish to the merchants, who get it loaded in trucks, which trundle it during the night to Madrid, where it will be served for lunch the following day. Columbus sailed from this port on his second voyage, and the scene can't have changed much. Across the bay is some of Europe's last wilderness, an enormous bird sanctuary and game preserve owned by some of the Sherry firms and various members of the nobility. It is occasionally hunted in the fall, from horseback, and lucky guests say they have never had such shooting, because it is on the flyway from northern Europe to Africa. There are boar and deer in the thickets, and herds of wild camels and horses, undisturbed except by the few game-keepers and the rare hunting party.

Spanish tourists visit Jerez to taste the wines, but few from other countries seem to manage. All the firms have regular tours of the bodegas, the great warehouses where the wines are stored. Sherries are always blended, even a *fino* taking seven years to mature, and nowhere else can you taste such Sherries because most of them are softened and sweetened before shipping overseas, an old tradition in the trade. The Spanish prefer them dry.

Even rarer than unsweetened Sherries are wines from the small district of Montilla, some fifty miles away. Like Sherries, the tumultuous fermentation is allowed to sub-side before the addition of brandy, so that the wine can be stabilized at the desired point of excellence. Like the *finos* and *amontillados*, they taste best perhaps with *ser-rano*, the air-dried ham from the mountains.

Much of the Sherry is shipped to London for bottling, another old tradition in the trade, and the casks make their way to Scotland and Ireland where they are used to age whiskies, the Sherry-soaked butts adding richness to the young spirit.

Custard of Jerez, called *flan*, is made with equal amounts of Sherry, sugar, and egg yolks, the whites being used to filter the wine. It is sometimes thin, and used on fruits or cakes, sometimes allowed to cook until it is thick, a thin *flan* being poured over the molded one. With coffee and a soft *oloroso*, you have a perfect Spanish ending to a meal.

Jerez makes brandies from its wines, brandies that are full and pungent and need long years in cask to develop. An old Spanish brandy is nothing like Cognac, but is distinguished in its own right, its heady taste being preferred by the Spanish to the delicacy of the French brandies. Many of the Sherry firms are now making light-colored, intense brandies distilled at a high proof, not so pungent as the traditional ones, but beginning to be known on the international markets. The pronounced tastes are popular with those who are tiring of overlight spirits.

There are many sweets in Spain, among them the jelly roll called Gypsy's Arm, a variety of meringues sold by various names in the bakeries of Andalusia, and many kinds of almond cakes. There are all kinds of fruit tarts and fritters, and chestnuts are prepared in many ways, including a soufflé. The jams are often too sugary, but there's a Seville special that is not, made from strips of pumpkin and called Angel's Hair. Then there's Cold Love, sliced fruits sugared and soaked in brandy, then chilled in a cream like *flan* to which gelatin has been added, then folded together with whipped cream and chilled. Fried milk is made by simmering milk with sugar, vanilla, and some flour paste, then chilling and dipping squares into egg, then bread crumbs, and sautéeing the slices in butter. It is served hot, after sprinkling with sugar.

Iberia is a land of contrasts, say the travel books, meaning that there are lots of poor people, so the governments run inns in the countryside, *paradores* or *posadas*, made over from castles, convents, and such, beautiful and ancient, if insulated, serving international meals and some local specialties to keep you interested. The cities have some marvelous hotels, like the Ritz or Palace in Madrid, the enormous Alfonso XIII in Sevilla, the new Ritz in Lisbon and the ancient Infanta de Sagres in Porto, all places to eat or have a drink in, even if you don't stay there. The coast resorts along the Costa Brava, around Málaga, on Majorca and the other Balearics, around San Sebastian, have all sorts of places for tourists, as do Cascais, Nazaré, and the rest of the Portugese coast. Spain is big, twice the size of the British Isles or West Germany, about as big as the Atlantic states from Maine to Virginia, with half of Pennsylvania thrown in, but with scarcely thirty million people. Crossed by mountains, it's a rumpled hide broiling in the summer sun, the reason why people eat lightly during the day, have a late lunch and nap, and dine in the cool of night. The cave country in the north, Altamira west of Santander, and Basondo near Bilbao, has seaside summer weather, but chill and misty winters. The Portugese coast is also hot, Iberia being most pleasant early in spring or late in fall.

Both countries devour enormous amounts of salt cod and a Portuguese cookbook will have dozens of ways to prepare *bacalhau,* many of them good. Portugal, particularly, is a place for fresh fish from the morning's catch,

broiled sardines dribbled with fresh olive oil, hake, sea
bass, oysters, lobsters, crab. The country is full of local
hams, particularly the northern Chaves and Lamego; slices
are often laid on sautéed beef to produce *bife portugués*,
and there's no better place to try it than in Oh Lacerda!
in Lisbon. The pork dishes are good, too, and at the Aviz
in Lisbon, which is one of the world's great restaurants,
you can get the national dish. *Carne de porco com ameijoas*
is a dice of quickly sautéed pork filet braised in white
wine, with unshucked clams.

Half a dozen years ago the national tourist office decided Portuguese restaurants were ignoring national
dishes, so they ruled that every eating place must feature
at least one national dish a day. Now it's easy to find the
codfish or shrimp cakes, the croquettes of fish, sea food or
chicken, the cheesecakes called *queijadas de sintra*, the
chickpea cakes called *azevias transmontanas*, and the
beancakes of Torres Vedras. The local cheeses are much
better and more varied than most of those in Spain, and
there are even more sweets, mostly custards and others
made from almond paste, not the least interesting being
Nun's Breasts, *papos de freira*. Nuns still make the sugar-
plums for Christmas, and the stuffed candied fruits are
everywhere.

The country is full of wines, Dão and Colares in the
south, *Vinho Verde* from the north, called green wine
because the reds, whites, and rosés are generally drunk
young, although some are better when a year or two
old. They are just right to drink in Lisbon's *fado* night-
clubs, many of which also serve pretty good food.

The great wine of Portugal is Port, named after the
four-thousand-year-old city that also named the country.

The wines are stored in lodges in Vila Nova de Gaia, just across the Douro river from the city, reached by bridges high above the deep gorge. All the famous firms welcome visitors. But the place to go is up the River of Gold, to the vineyards around Pinhão and Régua.

The mountains that run down to the river must have been molten once because they seem to have dried wrinkled, deep cuts and gouges reaching back into the land, their edges smoothed by time. Rivulets and pools course the vales. Paths slant up the banks to the dark cypresses on the ridges, like landscapes in Chinese paintings.

The river's course is flung open to the sky at Régua, and the broad, canted flanks of the hills are terraced all the way to Pinhão, with scorched patches here and there where the plantings were destroyed three generations ago by the phylloxera, a burrowing louse imported to Europe on American vine stocks. The bare patches were too costly to replant with grafted stocks, European vines on American roots, so these patches remain. The vineyards are still tended by hand, although some are open and flat enough to use animals.

Men bring the grapes to stone troughs in the vineyard pressing shed in the fall, and they are trod for hours as the juice runs, in time to singing or the strum of a guitar. The fermentation is stopped by dumping brandy into the fermenting butts of wine, to preserve some of the natural grape sweetness; then the slow aging begins.

Young Ports are ruby in color, changing to what is called tawny as they age. In a particularly good year, some of the wine is bottled promptly, to become Vintage Port, which may still be ruby in color after twenty years in bottle, when it begins to be opened for drinking. Various Rubies are blended together to make a bottling, as are various Tawnies, and these two are the wines usually drunk. The old custom of drinking Port after dinner or lunch still prevails in Porto, the men eating nuts or a Portuguese sweet like guava jelly, the bottle passing clockwise around the table, with the sun, until someone suggests they join the ladies. The wines, like Sherries, never die, simply becoming more intense and paralyzingly metallic to the tongue as the years go by, but these old stocks, of which every house has a few butts, are what give character to the blends.

No wine is better with melons or with custardy and sugary pastries, especially the almond-flavored ones so popular in Portugal.

The island of Madeira, out in the Atlantic off the African coast, makes a similar wine fortified with brandy, once immensely popular in colonial America but now rarely drunk. This trade, too, like that of Port and Sherry, has been strongly in English hands for over two centuries. There are many native families in the fortified wine trade, particularly in the Spanish Sherry trade, but even the Spanish and Portuguese families speak fluent English, the children frequently going to school in England. The popularity of these wines is gradually dwindling around the world, in the case of Madeira because quality has declined, in the case of Sherry because the shippers insist on sweetening their wines for a generation that prefers drinks dry, and in the case of Port because the government is jealous of the English control of the trade, wishing to consolidate it in Portuguese hands before promoting the wine. The trade likes to lament about the old days, when the three wines were a commonplace in any good Victorian household, always brought when guests arrived for tea. Their high cost today puts such niceties beyond the reach of many, to say nothing of the fact that people now ask for a cocktail or highball, so that a generation or two has grown up without knowing of the pleasures of a glass of well-chilled *fino* after a busy day, a sip of Madeira with a bite of cake, a glass of Port with some walnuts after dinner. But the Iberian peninsula shows signs of coming to life again on the European scene, thanks largely to the spirit of a brave people and a growing appreciation of things Iberian by a generation of holiday travelers, so the brave wines, too, may find new places on modern tables. At least the wine trade hopes so, and the wines are there, waiting to be welcomed.

APPENDIX

Some Books for a Wine Journey,
& Local Listings

In the old days of Edward and Victoria, the British wine merchants made annual wine journeys through France. Taking the boat train to Paris, after a few days they would head for Chartres and the cellars of the Loire valley, then proceed via Cognac to Bordeaux, then go down to Biarritz to rest up for a few days. Passing through the Armagnac country, they'd then head for Marseilles, stopping at Châteauneuf du Pape and Tavel before relaxing again on the Riviera. They'd then head for Aix and go up the Rhône and into Burgundy, then proceed on to Champagne and back to Paris, arriving home in London six weeks or so later, somewhat aglaze, a few pounds heavier, and much more content than when they started, but full of excuses for the rising prices of the vintages they'd bought.

Sometimes a merchant made the Grand Tour clockwise, arriving in Beaune for the auction at the Hospices on the third Sunday in November. Spring trips followed the same clockwise pattern, often preceded by a trip up the Rhine that included Alsace as the first French stop before Champagne. The trip was mostly unnecessary, because the merchant had been buying from the same firms for generations, and before he started he was pretty sure from advance reports which vintages he'd buy in Bordeaux, Rhône and Burgundy. Walter Berry wrote a book about such a trip in the thirties, with the advent of the motor car—he called it his "Little Auk"—which enabled him to break the pattern a little, making two trips to Burgundy, and including the Savoie. The book is a preposterous delight if you don't get too impatient with it, and it's called *In Search of Wine*. One morning in Reims a dozen years ago I saw such a couple preparing for the day's journey. They'd obviously been through the Champagne cellars the day before, because a porter was carefully packing an ice chest in the trunk of the Rolls, wedging it between the suitcases so it wouldn't tip over. Another porter stood by with the picnic hamper, to which was strapped a long French bread, wrapped in a checkered tablecloth. "In Chablis in time for dinner, if we don't stop too long for lunch," said the man to his companion. "I hope you've put the tea where you can get at it."

A few years before, a Frenchman had become distressed at the gradual disappearance of the French regional dishes and determined to make a record of them before they all disappeared into the stew of international cuisine. Wine and food producers all over France helped him to produce what may be for lovers of France and good food one of the saddest books ever written, Austin de Croze's *What to Eat and Drink in France*. Ardent optimists insist that not half, not even a third, possibly only a quarter, maybe only ten per cent of these dishes have disappeared or changed for the worse in the past thirty years. Among them is Waverley Root, who wrote a wonderful but briefer paean in a larger format five years ago, *The Food of France*. The best way to see for yourself is to buy this year's Michelin.

The Michelin guides are the best in the world, not just for France, but also for Spain, Italy, Switzerland, and the other countries of Europe. They list hotels and restaurants, including specialties, but they refrain from judging those in foreign lands too precisely, except to indicate those that are better than average. Swiss wine and food lovers also produce a quarterly that rates restaurants, called *Plaisirs*, whose address is Colombier, Neuchâtel, a subscription costing seven and a half Swiss francs for four issues, or less than two dollars. It's in French, but the listings are easy to read. For about the same price, the Touring Club Italiano publishes each year a guide similar to Michelin, called the *Vademecum*, which lists specialties, and uses two stars for outstanding restaurants (*cucina ottima*), one star for superior ones (*cucina molto buona*). In England, the best guide is Postgate's, which also includes a section on Ireland.

The tourist offices of the various countries print restaurant lists, and any native can tick off in a couple of minutes the ones not to miss. Those for Vienna, Brussels, Amsterdam, Copenhagen, and Stockholm are particularly good. Most of the big cities have handout periodicals or folding pocket cards that are given away in the palace hotels, and these can be useful, while SAS, the Scandinavian air line, publishes pocket folders for most of the leading European cities, which include a map of the town and notes on restaurants, hotels, shopping and tours. The wise traveler pays a visit to the local tourist office as soon as he arrives in a city, to pick up the week's calendar of events, street maps, and whatever else is momentarily available, then stops in at American Express to see if there's any mail and to check out the town with compatriots who've been around for a few days. This is a good way to shake off the inertia that comes from travel shock, that numbing confusion and timidity resulting from traveling too far, too fast, in lands where all is strange.

It was an Irishman who told me the best place in any foreign country to get information is the local American consulate or embassy, a fact that's well known to lots of Europeans but which never seems to cross an American's mind unless he wants to do business with the locals. I've had good luck with local Chambers of Commerce and with national tourist offices, which are set up to help the visitor, and sometimes can.

The national airports and main railroad stations invariably contain a bureau for locating hotel rooms, and they do wonders even in the height of the season.

Glossary of food & wine terms

English RESTAURANT	French RESTAURANT	Italian RISTORANTE	Spanish RESTORÁN	German RESTAURANT
the menu	la carte	la lista	la lista de platos	die Speisekarte
waiter	garçon	cameriere	camarero	Kellner
napkin	serviette	tovagliolo	servilleta	Serviette
knife	couteau	coltello	cuchillo	Messer
fork	fourchette	forchetta	tenedor	Gabel
spoon	cuiller	cucchiaio	cuchara	Löffel
plate	plat	piatto	plato	Teller
cup	tasse	tazza	taza	Tasse
glass	verre	bicchiere	vaso	Glas
appetizer	hors-d'œuvre	antipasto	aperitivo *or* entremés	Vorspeise
bread	pain	pane	pan	Brot
butter	beurre	burro	mantequilla	Butter
toast	pain grillé	pane abbrustolito	tostado	Röstbrot
marmalade	marmelade	marmellata	mermelada	Marmelade
ice cream	glace	gelato	helado	Gefrorenes
breakfast	petit déjeuner	prima colazione	desayuno	Frühstück
lunch	déjeuner	colazione	almuerzo *or* merienda	Gabelfrühstück *or* Mittagessen
dinner	diner	pranzo	comida	Abendessen
Some more, please.	Encore, s'il vous plait.	Ancora, prego.	Más, por favor.	Noch einmal, bitte.
The check, please.	L'addition, s'il vous plait.	Il conto, per piacere.	La cuenta, por favor.	Geben Sie mir die Rechnung, bitte.
Is the tip included?	Le service est-il compris?	Il servizio è incluso?	¿Esta incluída la propina?	Ist die Bedienung eingerechnet?

English BEVERAGES	French BOISSONS	Italian BEVERAGGI	Spanish BEBIDAS	German GETRANKE
beer	bière	birra	cervesa	Bier
coffee	café	caffé	café	Kaffee
cream	crème	panna	crema	Sahne
whipped	crème fouettée	panna montata	crema batida	Schlagsahne
milk	lait	latte	leche	Milch
orange juice	jus d'orange	sugo d'arancia	jugo de naranja	Orangensaft
tea	thé	te	té	Tee
wine	vin	vino	vino	Wein

English	French	Italian	Spanish	German
EGGS	ŒUFS	UOVA	HUEVOS	EIER

English	French	Italian	Spanish	German
fried eggs	œufs sur le plat *or* œufs frits	uova nel tegame *or* fritte	huevos fritos	Spiegeleier
hard-boiled eggs	œufs durs	uova sode	huevos duros	hartgekochte Eier
soft-boiled eggs	œufs à la coque	uova a bere	huevos pasados por agua	weichgekochte Eier
omelet	omelette	frittata	tortilla de huevos	Eierkuchen
poached eggs	œufs pochés	uova affogate	escalfados	verlorene Eier
scrambled eggs	œufs brouillés	uova strapazzate	huevos revueltos	Rühreier

English	French	Italian	Spanish	German
MEAT	VIANDE	CARNE	CARNE	FLEISCH

English	French	Italian	Spanish	German
brains	cervelles	cervelli	sesos	Gehirne
breast	poitrine	petto	pecho	Brust
brisket	poitrine	petto	pecho	Bruststück
chops *or* cutlets	côtelettes	costolette	chuletas	Rippchen
haunch	hanche	anca	anca	Hüfte
head	tête	testa	cabeza	Kopf
heart	cœur	cuore	corazón	Herz
joint	grosse pièce	taglio	cuarto de una res	Braten
kidneys	rognons	rognone	riñones	Nieren
leg	gigot	coscia	pata	Keule *or* Schlagel
liver	foie	fegato	hígado	Leber
loin	longe	lombata	lomo	Lende
marrow	moelle	midollo	médula	Mark
neck	cou	collo	cuello	Hals
rib	côte	costola	costilla	Rippe
roast	rôti	arrosto	asado	Braten
round	rouelle	rotolo	lomo	Rinderkeule
rump	culotte	culaccio	solomo	Schwanzstück
saddle	selle	schiena	lomo	Rücken
shoulder	épaule	spalla	espaldilla	Schulter
skin	peau	pelle	piel	Haut
slice	tranche	fetta	tajada	Schnitte
sweetbread	ris	animella	lechecillas	Bröschen
tongue	langue	lingua	lengua	Zunge
bacon	lard	lardo	tocino	Speck
beef	bœuf	manzo *or* bue	carne de vaca	Rindfleisch
oxtail	queue de bœuf	coda di bue	cola de vaca	Ochsenschwanz
steak	bifteck	bistecca	bistec	Steak
rare	*saignant*	*all'inglese*	*a la inglesa*	*englisch*
medium	à *point*	*al punto*	*mediano*	*halb durchgebraten*
well done	*bien cuit*	*ben cotta*	*a la española*	*gut durchgebraten*

(CONTINUED)

English MEAT	French VIANDE	Italian CARNE	Spanish CARNE	German FLEISCH
ham	jambon	prosciutto	jamón	Schinken
lamb	agneau	agnello	carne de cordero	Lamm
mutton	mouton	castrato	carne de carnero	Hammelfleisch
pork	porc	porco *or* maiale	puerco	Schweinefleisch
veal	veau	vitello	ternera	Kalbfleisch

English FOWL AND GAME	French VOLAILLE ET GIBIER	Italian POLLAME E SELVAGGINA	Spanish AVES DE CORRAL Y CAZA	German GEFLÜGEL UND WILDBRET
boar	sanglier	cignale	jabalí	Wildschwein
young	marcassin	cinghialetto	jabato	Frischling
capon	chapon	cappone	alcarab	Kapaun
chick	poussin	pulcino	polluelo	Küchlein
chicken	poulet	pollo	pollo	Huhn
spring	poulet de grain	galletto	pollo tierno	junges Huhn
roasting		pollo per arrosto	pollo para asar	Brathuhn
pullet	poularde	pollastra	————	Hühnchen
hen	poule	gallina	gallina	Huhn
liver	foie de volaille	fegato di pollo	higado de pollo	Hühnerleber
deer	cerf	cervo	ciervo	Hirsch
duck	canard	anitra	pato	Ente
wild	canard sauvage	anitra selvatica	pato silvestre	Wildente
duckling	caneton	anatrino	anadino	Entchen
figpecker	becfigue	beccafico	papfigo	Feigendrossel
goose	oie	oca	ganso	Gans
gosling	oison	papero	ansarón	Gänschen
grouse	tétras	gallo di montagna	guaco	Birkhuhn
guinea fowl	pintade	gallina faraona	pintada	Perlhuhn
hare	lièvre	lepre	liebre	Hase
young	levraut	leprotto	liebrezuela	Häschen
hazel hen	gelinotte des bois	gallina regina	ortega	Haselhuhn
heath cock	coq de bruyère	urogallo	urogallo	Auerhahn *or* Birkhahn
lark	mauviette	allodola	alondra	Lerche
partridge	perdreau	pernice	perdiz	Rebhuhn *or* Feldhuhn
young	perdrix	perniciotto	perdigón	————
peacock	paon	pavone	pavo real	Pfau

(CONTINUED)

English FOWL AND GAME	French VOLAILLE ET GIBIER	Italian POLLAME E SELVAGGINA	Spanish AVES DE CORRAL Y CAZA	German GEFLÜGEL UND WILDBRET
pheasant	faisan	fagiano	faisán	Fasan
pigeon	pigeon	piccione	paloma	Taube
plover *or* lapwing	pluvier *or* vanneau	vanello	avefría	Kiebitz
quail	caille	quaglia	codorniz	Wachtel
rabbit	lapin	coniglio	conejo	Kaninchen
young	lapereau	———	———	junges Kaninchen
roebuck	chevreuil	capriolo	corzo	Rehbock
snipe	bécassine	beccaccia	becada	Schnepfe
squab	pigeonneau	piccionello	pichón	junge Taube
teal	sarcelle	arzavola	cerceta	Krickente
thrush	grive	tordo	tordo	Drossel
turkey	dinde	tacchino	pava	Puter
young	dindonneau	tacchino giovane	pavipollo	junger Puter
venison	venaison	cervo *or* daino	venado	Wildbret
woodcock	bécasse	beccaccia	urogallo	Waldschnepfe

English FISH	French POISSON	Italian PESCE	Spanish PESCADO	German FISCH
anchovy	anchois	accuighe	anchoa	Anchovis *or* Sardelle
bass	bar	pesce	róbalo	Barsch
cod, fresh	cabillaud	merluzzo	bacalao	Kabeljau
eel	anguille	anguilla	anguila	Aal
flounder	flet *or* carrelet	passerino	lenguado	Flunder
haddock	aiglefin	nasello	merluza	Schellfisch
halibut	flétan	passera	hipogloso	Heilbutte
herring	hareng	aringa	arenque	Hering
mackerel	maquereau	sgombro	escombro	Makrele
mullet, red	rouget	triglia	barbo de mar	Meerbarbe
perch-pike	sandre	luccioperca	lucio	Zander
pike	brochet	luccio	lucio	Hecht
pollock	colin	nasello	abadejo	Pollack
roe	œufs de poisson	uova di pesce	huevas de pescado	Fischrogen
salmon	saumon	salmone	salmón	Lachs *or* Salm
shad	alose	alosa	sábalo *or* alosa	Alse
sole	sole	sogliola	lenguado	Seezunge
sturgeon	esturgeon	storione	esturión	Stör
trout	truite	trota	trucha	Forelle
tuna	thon	tonno	atún	Thunfisch
turbot	turbot	rombo	rodaballo	Steinbutte

English SHELLFISH	*French* CRUSTACÉS	*Italian* CROSTACEI MOLLUSCHI	*Spanish* MARISCOS	*German* SCHALTIERE
crab	crabe	granchio	cangrejo	Krabbe *or* Krebs
crawfish *or* spiny lobster	langouste	aragosta	langosta	Heuschrecken-krebs
crayfish	écrivisse	gambero	langostino	Flusskrebs
frogs' legs	cuisses de grenouille	gambe di ranocchie	patas de rana	Froschschenkel
lobster	homard	gambero di mare	langosta	Hummer
mussels	moules	cozze	mejillones	Muscheln
oysters	huitres	ostriche	ostras	Austern
prawns	crevettes roses *or* langoustines	gamberetti di mare	gambas	Steingarnelen
scallops	coquilles St.-Jacques	pettonchi	veneras	Kammuscheln
sea urchin	oursin	echino *or* riccio marino	erizo de mar	Seeigel
shrimp	crevettes grises	gamberettini	camarones	Garnelen
snails	escargots	lumache	caracoles	Schnecken
squid	calmar	calamaro	calamares	Tintenfisch

English VEGETABLES	*French* LÉGUMES	*Italian* LEGUMI	*Spanish* LEGUMBRES	*German* GEMÜSE
artichoke	artichaut	carciofi	alcachofa	Artichocke
asparagus	asperges	asparagi	espárragos	Spargel
beans				
kidney	féveroles	fagioli	frijoles	Schminkbohnen
string,	haricots	fagioli bianchi	judías blancas	weisse Bohnen
dried	haricots verts	fagiolini	habichuelas	grüne Bohnen
green				
beetroot	betterave	barbabietola	remolacha	rote Rübe
broccoli	brocoli	broccoli	bróculi	Spargelkohl
cabbage	chou	cavolo	col	Kohl *or* Kraut
carrot	carotte	carota	zanahoria	Mohrrübe *or* Karotte
cauliflower	chou-fleur	cavolfiore	coliflor	Blumenkohl
celery	céleri	sedano	apio	Sellerie
corn	mais	granturco	maíz	Mais
cucumber	concombre	cetriolo	pepino *or* cohombro	Gurke
eggplant	aubergine	melanzana	berenjena	Eierpflanze
endive	endive	indivia	endibia	Endivie
kale	chou vert	cavolo riccio	bretón	Grünkohl
leeks	poireaux	porri	puerros	Lauch
lentils	lentilles	lenticchie	lentejas	Linsen
lettuce	laitue	lattuga	lechuga	Kopfsalat *or* Lattich

(CONTINUED)

English VEGETABLES	French LÉGUMES	Italian LEGUMI	Spanish LEGUMBRES	German GEMÜSE
mushrooms	champignons	funghi	hongos	Pilze
parsnip	panais	pastinaca	chirivia	Pastinake
peas	petits pois	piselli	guisantes	Erbsen
pepper, green	poivron *or* piment doux	peperone	pimiento	Paprikaschote
potato	pomme de terre	patata	patata	Kartoffel
pumpkin	citrouille	zucca	calabaza	Kürbis
radish	radis	rapanello	rábano	Rettich
rhubarb	rhubarbe	rabarbaro	ruibarbo	Rhabarber
sorrel	oseille	acetosella	acedera	Sauerampfer
spinach	épinard	spinace	espinaca	Spinat
squash	courgette	zucchini	calabaza	Melonenkürbis
tomato	tomate	pomodoro	tomate	Tomate
truffles	truffes	tartufi	trufas	Trüffeln
turnip	navet	navone *or* rapa	nabo	Rübe

English HERBS SPICES SEASONING	French HERBES ÉPICES ASSAISONNE- MENT	Itallian ERBE SPEZIE CONDIMENTO	Spanish HIERBAS ESPECIA CONDIMENTO	German KRAUTER GEWÜRZE WÜRZE
capers	câpres	capperi	alcaparras	Kapern
caraway	carvi	seme di carvi	alcaravea	Kümmel
cinnamon	cannelle	cannella	canela	Zimt
clove	girofle	garofalo	clavos	Gewürznelke
coriander	coriandre	corandolo	cilantro	Koriander
garlic	ail	aglio	ajo	Knoblauch
ginger	gingembre	zenzero	jengibre	Ingwer
horseradish	raifort	ramolaccio	rábano picante	Meerrettich
mustard	moutarde	senapa	mostaza	Senf
nutmeg	noix de muscade	noce moscada	nuez moscada	Muskatnuss
parsley	persil	prezzemolo	perejil	Petersilie
pepper	poivre	pepe	pimienta	Pfeffer
peppermint	menthe	menta pepata	hierbabuena	Pfefferminze
sage	sauge	salvia	salvia	Salbei
salt	sel	sale	sal	Salz
sugar	sucre	zucchero	azúcar	Zucker
tarragon	estragon	targone	estragón	Estragon
thyme	thym	timo	tomillo	Thymian
vinegar	vinaigre	aceto	vinagre	Essig

English NUTS AND FRUITS	*French* NOIX ET FRUITS	*Italian* NOCI E FRUTTA	*Spanish* NUECES Y FRUTAS	*German* NÜSSE UND FRÜCHTE
almond	amande	mandorla	almendra	Mandel
apple	pomme	mela	manzana	Apfel
apricot	abricot	albicocca	albaricoque	Aprikose
avocado	avocat	pera avvocato	aguacate	Flaschenbirne
blackberries	mûres de ronce	more di rovo	zarzamoras	Brombeeren
cantaloupe	cantaloup	meloncini	cantalú	Warzenmelone
cherries	cerises	ciliegie	cerezas	Kirschen
chestnut	marron	castagno	castaña	Kastanie
coconut	noix de coco	noce di cocco	coco	Kokosnuss
currants	groseilles	ribes rosso	grosellas	Johannisbeeren
dates	dattes	datteri	dátiles	Datteln
fig	figue	fico	higo	Feige
filbert	aveline	nocciola	avellana	Haselnuss
gooseberries	groseilles à maquereau	ribes	uva espina	Stachelbeeren
grapefruit	pamplemousse	pampelimosa	toronja	Pompelmuse
grapes	raisins	uve	uvas	Trauben
huckleberries	myrtilles	mirtilli	arándano	Heidelbeeren
lemon	citron	limone	limón	Zitrone
lime	limon	lima	lima	Süsszitrone
medlar	nêfle	nespola	níspera	Mispel
mulberries	mûres	more	moras	Maulbeeren
nectarine	brugnon	pesca noce	abridor	Nektarinen-pfirsich
orange	orange	arancia	naranja	Apfelsine
peach	pêche	pesca	melocotón	Pfirsich
pineapple	ananas	ananasso	piña	Ananas
pistachio	pistache	noce di pistacchio	alfóncigo	Pistazie
plum	prune	ciruela	prugna	Pflaume
pomegranate	grenade	granada	melagrana	Granatapfel
quince	coing	membrillo	cotogna	Quitte
raspberries	framboises	frambuesas	lamponi	Himbeeren
strawberries	fraises	fresas	fragole	Erdbeeren
walnut	noix	nueces	noce	Walnuss

List of food & beverage organizations

NOTE: The customary way of writing addresses varies from country to country. The forms listed here have been received from the individual company or its importer, and are the ones that promise most rapid delivery.

All firms listed have indicated a willingness to welcome visitors, but it is best to request or announce a visit in writing, two weeks before; the more specific you can be about times, the better. Enclose an addressed postcard if you wish confirmation. Where the phone is listed, a call before visiting is enough to confirm an appointment.

Best days are the middle of the week, generally after ten in the morning, after two in the afternoon. Many firms have skeleton staffs during the summer months, particularly during August. Fall and spring are the best seasons for visiting.

FRANCE

Foods

CANDIES

Bonbons Barnier, 35 rue des Emmurées, Rouen.

Choco Paris, 55 Quai de Seine, Paris.

Dubayon & Brulin, 50 rue des Francs-Bourgeois, Paris.

Manufacture Parisienne de Confiserie (Bonbons "Tour Eiffel"), 155 Bd. Dávóut, Paris.

Poulain (Chocolaterie-confiserie), Blois (Loire et Cher).

John Tavernier, 1 rue du Cloitre St.-Merri, Paris.

Usine Nestlé de Gap, Hautes-Alpes.

CANNED SPECIALTIES

Amieux, 25 rue de Chevreul, Nantes (L.A.).

Ets. Barbier-Dauphin, 4 Place Jeanne d'Arc, Aix-en-Provence.

Cassegrain, 341 Route de Clisson, Saint Sebastien s/Loire (L.A.).

Feyel, 27 rue du Dome, Strasbourg.

Gillot, Vallentigny, Hampigny (Aube).

Ste.-Française du Graal, 8 rue Reaumur, Nantes (L.A.).

Joubert-Narcy, 100 rue Jeanne d'Arc, Chatellerault.

Leymarie, Mont de Marsan (Landes).

Ets. V.J.F.-Malvoisin, Port Fluvial, Macon. Paris Office: 149, Ave. Paul-Vaillant-Couturier, Gentilly (Seine). Tél.: Alesia 24–36.

Milliat Freres, 31 rue Lavoisier, Nanterre (Seine).

Conserves Pebeyre, Cours de la Chartreuse, Cahors.

Petit Jean Gay, 22 rue Gabriel Peri, Pre Saint Gervais (Seine).

Pien et Glasson, Beuvillers par Lisieux (Calvados).

Quenelles Rack, Dijon (Cote d'Or).

Raphalen, Ploneour-Lanvern (Finistere).

Raynal et Roquelaure, Capdenac (Aveyron).

Rougie Vivies, Calviac (Dordogne).

La Semeuse, Bergues (Nord).

CHEESE & DAIRY PRODUCTS

Ets Barthelemy, rue de la Poterie, Paris.

Fromageries Bel, 4 rue d'Anjou, Paris.

Laiterie Durand, Thiaucourt (Meurthe & Moselle).

Moutarde Grey-Poupon, 94 rue Jean-Jaure, Levallois.

Normandie-Lait, Saint Pierre s/Devis (Calvados).

Moutarde Parizot, 15 Bd. Georges Clemenceau, Dijon.

Société Agricole de Roquefort, Roquefort (Aveyron).

Fromageries Victor Renaut, 41 avenue General Leclerc, Doue
   La Fontaine (Meuse & Loire).

S.A.F.R. (Ste.-Anonyme des Fermiere Reunis), 44 rue Louis
   Blanc, Paris.

Laiterie St-Hubert, 17/27 rue Pichon, St-Hubert (Seine &
   Oise).

Négobeureuf, 7 rue de la Poterie, Paris 1. Tél.. GUT 55.01.

Laiterie Moderne de la Roche Etroite, Busseau (Creuse).

Laiterie Moderne du Rocher, Savigne-l'Eveque (Sarthe).

Damilait, Damigni (Orne).

Laiterie Moderne de Redon, Redon.

CHESTNUTS

Syndicat de Défense des Marrons des Maures, M. Perrin, Les
   Mayons, Var.

COOKIES

Biscuits Belin, 10 rue H. Petit, Chateau-Thierry (Aisne).

Biscuits Brossard, 40 Bd. Lair, St.-Jean d'Angely (Ch. Mme).

Biscuits Brun, 26 rue Mederic, Maisons-Alfort (Seine).

Damoy (Ets Julien), 31 Bd. de Sebastopol, Paris.

Biscottes Darry, Pierrecourt par Nesle Normandeuse.

Dupont d'Isigny, 66, Bd. Bineau, Neuilly.

Maison Paul Etienne Pere & Fils, St-Peray (Ardeche).

Eubeurlay (Ste.-Ciale des Specialtes), Ampuis (Rhone).

Ets Geslot-Woreux, Boite Postale No. 13, Ronchin (Nord).

Grellier, (Biscuits St-Michel), Saint Michel, Chefchef (L.A.).

Lefévre-Utile, Quai Baco, Nantes (L.A.).

Biscuits Nantes (B.N.), Place Francois II, Nantes (L.A.).

Biscottes Pelletier, 66 rue de la Fraternite, Romainville (Seine).

Biscuits Perroneau, 20 rue du Fg. Raines, Dijon (Cote d'Or).

Biscottes Prior, 73 Bd. de St-Marcel, Marseilles.

Maîtres Biscottiers Reunis, 21 rue Joseph Doury, **Nantes** (L.A.).

Biscuits Rogeron, 70/82, rue Lesage, Reims.

Ets Roulambert, Savigny Les Beaune (Cote d'Or).

Nicol Tanguy, 29 Bd. de Kerguelen, Quimper.

Unimel, 164 avenue de Neuilly, Neuilly a/Seine.

Foie Gras and Gooseliver

Georges Bruck, 7, Rue Friese, Strasbourg (Bas-Rhin). **Days** & Hours: Mon.–Fri. 9–12, 2–4. Phone: 33-00-72.

Louis Henry, 35 rue du Faubourg de Pierre Strasbourg.

Et's. Rouges Vivies, Souillac (Lot). 48 hrs. advance **notice** required.

Fruits and Vegetables

HAUTES ALPES

Coopérative Fruitière de Laragne.

PROVENCE

Coopérative de Fruits & Légumes "L'Arlésienne," **Arles** (B.D.R.), Président M. Joseph Simian. Tél.: 14.97.

Coopérative de Fruits & Légumes "Le Grand Rhône," Le Sambuc (B.D.R.), Directeur M. de Villeneuve. Tél.: 004.

Coopérative de Fruits "Les Vergers de Cabannes," Cabannes (B.D.R.), Président M. Tamisier. Tél.: 079.

Coopérative de Fruits "Les Vergers de St. Andiol," St. Andiol (B.D.R.), Directeur M. Gilles. Tél.: 087.

Coopérative de Fruits "La Muscadelle" à St. Andiol (B.D.R.), Directeur M. Bruneau. Tél.: 42.

Coopérative de Fruits et Légumes de St. Rémy (B.D.R.), Président, M. Jean Desfonts. Tél.: 113.

Coopérative de Fruits "Les Verges de Senas," SENAS (B.D.R.). Tél.: 004.

Coopérative des Producteurs de Fruits et Légumes des B.D.R., Salon (B.D.R.), Directur M. Declary. Tél.: 157.

Coopérative de Fruits & Légumes "Provincia Fruits" à Orange, Vaucluse, Directeur M. Bérenger. Tél.: 939.

Coopérative de Conserves de Fruits & Légumes de Camaret, Vaucluse, Directeur M. Biscarat.

Coopérative de Fruits & Légumes "Provence Comtat," Le Thor, Vaucluse. Tél.: 83.21.66.

Coopérative de Fruits & Légumes Copildor, Quartier des deux gares à Hyères, Var. Tél.: 305.

MUSHROOMS

Et's. Blanchaud, Chace (Maine-et-Loire). N.Y. Rep.: *Bernard L. Lewis, Inc.,* Public Relations, Empire State Building, N.Y. 1.

MUSTARD

Grey et Poupon, Dijon. Arrangements made by the Syndicat d'Initiative, Pavillon du Tourisme, Place Darcy, Dijon.

OLIVES AND OLIVE OIL

Coopérative des Producteurs d'Olives et d'Huile d'Olives de France, Quartier Séloni, Aix, Provence. (B.D.R.), Directeur M. Paul. Tél.: 830.

PORK PRODUCTS

Mr. Gaston Deterville, Sec. Gen., Et's. Pien Glasson, Beauvillers par Lisieux (Calvados) Normandy (near Le Havre). Days & Hours: Mon.–Thurs. 8–11, 1:30–4:30.

Coopérative de conserve de viande "Le Pelican Blanc," Pelissanne (B.D.R.), Directeur M. Lyon. Tél.: 34.

RICE

Coopérative des Producteurs de Riz, Route de Tarascon, Arles (B.D.R.). Tél.: 189.

Coopérative de Riz des Alpes & Provence, Pont de Crau, Arles (B.D.R.). Directeur M Patissier. Tél.: 129.

Beer

Brasserie de Kronenbourg, Strasbourg-Kronenbourg.

Brasserie de l'Esperance, Schiltigheim, Strasbourg.

Spirits

Bénédictine, S.A. Producers of Benedictine liqueur and B&B liqueur. Fécamp, Normandy. Days & Hours: Mon.–Sat. 9–5. Visitors tour will include the Benedictine Abbey.

Les Fils de P. Bardinet, Boite Postale 513, Bordeaux.

Ste. des Produits Marnier-Lapostolle, 91, Boulevard Haussmann, Paris 8.

Cie Française de la Grande Chartreuse, B.P. 91, Voiron Chartreuse. Tel.: Voiron 1–73 and 93.

Et's. Combier, 48 Rue Beaurepaire, Saumur. Days & Hours: Mon.–Fri. 9–11:30, 2–6. (Liqueurs).

Maison Cointreau, Place Molière, Angers. Days & Hours: Mon.–Fri. 9–11, 2–4. (Liqueurs).

Marie Brizard & Roger S.A., 128–142 Rue Fondaudege, Bordeaux. Tel.: 52, 56, 80 to 85.

Liqueurs Dolfi, 19 Bd. President Wilson, Strassbourg.

Distillerie P. Garnier, Enghien les Bains, Seine-et-Oise.

Get Frères Revel, Haute-Garonne.

Distillerie De La Côte Basque (Liqueur Izarra), Quai Bergeret, Bayonne.

Messrs. G. A. Jourde (Cordial Medoc), Cenon, Gironde.

Ets J. and J. Pallas, Domaine de Cassanel, Nérac en Armagrac (Lot & Caronne).

COGNAC (CHARENTE)

Bureau National du Cognac, 3 rue Georges Briand, Cognac.

Bisquit Dubouche & Co., Quai de l'Orangerie, Jarnac.

Courvoisier Ltd., Place du Château, Jarnac.

Jas. Hennessey & Co., rue de la Richonne, Cognac. Tél.: 12 and 42.

E. Remy Martin & Co., 14 rue de la Société Vinicole, Cognac.

Denis-Mounie & Co., Cognac.

Martell & Co., Place Edouard Martell, Cognac.

Grand Empereur Napoleon, 4 rue Jean-Jaurès, Cognac.

Ets. Papelorey, Larressingle, Condom (Gers). Tél.: 33.

Cognac Prince de Polignac, 29 rue Lohmeyer, Cognac.

Jules Robin, 24 rue Gabriel Jaulin, Cognac.

Wines

COMITES INTERPROFESSIONNELS

Comité Interprofessionnel du Vin de Champagne, 5, rue Henri Martin, Epernay (Marne). Tél.: 990 à 993. Directeur de la Commission d'Information: M. Dargent. Directeur: M. Medard.

Conseil Interprofessionnel du Vin de Bordeaux, I, cours du XXX Juillet Bordeaux (Gde.) Tél.: 77–61. Président: M. Henri Martin. Directeur: M. Barailhe.

Conseil Interprofessionnel des Vins d'Anjou et de Saumur, 21 Bld. Foch, Angers (Maine et Loire). Tél.: 63–82. Président: M. Besombes. Directeur: M. Labbe.

Comité Interprofessionnel des Vins de Touraine, Chambre de Commerce, 12, rue Berthelot, Tours (Indre-&-Loire). Tél.: 32–24. Président: M. Robert Amirault. Secrétaire Général: M. Violette.

Comité Interprofessionnel des Vins d'Origine du Pays Nantais, 12, rue de Strasbourg, Nantes (Loire Atl.). Tél.: 159–82. Président: M. de Couesbouc.

Comité Interprofessionnel des Vins Doux Naturels, 2, rue Léon Dieudé, Perpignan (Pyr. O.). Tél.: 29–97. Président: M. Henry Vidal. Directeur: M. Mengaud.

Comité Interprofessionnel des Vins des Côtes-du-Rhône, 92, rue Joseph Vernet, Avignon (Vaucluse). Tél.: 24–64. Président: M. Albert Rieu. Directeur: M. Ligier.

Comité Interprofessionnel des Vins de Côtes-de-Provence, Boulevard Gambetta, Les Arcs (Var.). Tél.: 101. Président: M. Gérald Cassin.

Comité Interprofessionnel des Vins de Fitou, Corbières, Minervois, La Clape et Quatourze, Sous-Préfecture Narbonne. Président: M. Sirven. Directeur: M. de Lamy.

Bureau National de l'Armagnac, Place de la Liberté, Eauze (Gers). Tél.: 93. Directeur: M. Diris.

Bureau National du Cognac, 3. rue Georges Briand Cognac (Charente). Tél.: 8.88. Directeur: M. Coquillaud.

Union Interprofessionnelle des Vins du Beaujolais, II, rue de la Gare, Villefranche-Sur-Saône (Rhône). Président: M. Dupont.

Comité Interprofessionnel des Vins de Gaillac, Mairie de Gaillac, Gaillac (Tarn). Président: M. Jean Petit.

Comité Interprofessionnel des Vins due Mâconnais, Maison Mâconnaise des Vins à Mâcon (Saône-et-Loire).

Comité Interprofessionnel des Vins d'Alsace, 5, Place de la Gare Colmar (en formation).

Conseil Interprofessionnel des Vins de la Région de Bergerac, Place du Docteur Cayla Bergerac (Dordogne). Tél. 12.57. Président: M. Royere.

CONFRERIES VINEUSES

Confrérie Universelle et Militante des Chevaliers du Cep. M. Causse, Journée Vinicole, 7 rue Dom Vaissette, Montpellier (Hérault).

Confrérie des Sacavins d'Anjou, 21, Bd. Foch, Angers (Maine-&-Loire).

Confrérie des Chevaliers du Tastevin de Bourgogne, M. Rodier, Nuits-St. Georges (Côte d'Or).

Confrérie de St. Etienne d'Ammerswihr, 25 av. Foch, Colmar (Haut-Rhin).

Confrérie des Bretvins de Nantes, Syndicat du Gros Plant, 9, rue du Bon Secours, Nantes (Loire Atlantique).

Confrérie de la Chantepleure de Vouvray à Vouvray (Indre-&-Loire).

Compagnons du Beaujolais, M. Pluvy, St. Georges-de-Reneins (Rhône).

Jurade de Saint-Emilion à Saint-Emilion (Gironde).

Ordre des Compagnons du Bontemps du Médoc à Pauillac (Gironde).

Principauté de Franc-Pineau (Pineau des Charentes), 51, avenue Bugeaud, Paris (16e).

Compagnie des Mousquetaires d'Armagnac, Bl. Baston, Condom (Gers).

Confrérie des Baillis de Pouilly-sur-Loire, Pouilly-sur-Loire (Nièvre).

Ordre Illustre des Chevaliers de Méduse, M. A. Moréni, Palais de la Bourse, Bd. de Strasbourg, Toulon (Var.)

Connétablie de Guyenne (Ières Côtes de Bordeaux), M. Luccin, Tabanac (Gironde).

Viguerie Royale de Jurançon, Jurançon (Basses-Pyrénées) et: Maison du Paysan, Pau (Basses-Pyrénées).

Confrérie des Vignerons de St. Vincent (du Beaujolais), M. Chervet, Vire près Mâcon (Saône-&-Loire).

Confrérie Rabelaisienne de la Dive Bouteille de Gaillac, Gaillac (Tarn).

Confrérie des Tire-Douzils, M. Gérard Marot, 26, rue Alsace-Lorraine, Poitiers (Vienne). (Vins du Poitou).

Compagnons du Bouju, Caveau Jurassien, 30, rue Lecourbe, Lons-le-Saunier (Jura).

Le Consulat de Bergerac, Place du Dr. Cayla, Bergerac (Dordogne).

ALSACE

Groupement des Producteurs, Negociants Du Vignoble Alsacien, 1 Place de la Gare, Colmar. Days & Hours: Mon–Fri. 9–12, 2–5. Write 15 days in advance of visit.

Dopff and Irion, Riquewihr (Haut-Rhin). Oct. 10–Nov. 10 is the most interesting time of the year. This is when the gathering and pressing of the grapes can be seen by the visitor.

Dopff Au Molin, Riquewihr. Days & Hours: Daily, including Sundays and holidays. 8–6.

Edel Frères, Mittelwihr. Days & Hours: Daily, including Sundays and holidays. All day.

Hugel & Fils, Riquewihr. Days & Hours: Daily except Sat. afternoon and Sun. 9–6.

Eugene Klipfel, Barr. Days & Hours: Mon.–Fri. 9–12, 2–6.

Jules Muller & Fils, Bergheim. Days & Hours: Mon.–Fri. 8–12, 2–6. Also Sat. & Sun. if visits arranged in advance.

Domaines Viticoles Schlumberger, Guebwiller. Days & Hours: Mon.–Fri. 10–12, 2–5.

Adolphe Wilmm, Barr. Days & Hours: Daily except Sat. afternoon and Sun, 9–6.

Dolfi, 19 Blvd. Pres. Wilson, Strasbourg.

Brasserie de Kronenbourg, Strasbourg-Kronenbourg, Bas-Rhin.

ANJOU & SAUMUR

[For information, introductions, and visits to vineyards, address C.I.V.A.S., Maison du Vin d'Anjou, 21 Boulevard Foch, Angers.]

Emile Blanchard & Fils, Saint Lambert Du Lattay (Maine-et-Loire). N.Y. Rep.: *Monsieur Henri Wines, Ltd.*, 131 Morgan Ave., Brooklyn 37, N.Y.

Et's. A. Bescombes, St. Hilaire, St. Florent. Days & Hours: Mon.–Fri. 9–11:30, 2–6.

Et's. Remy-Pannier, St. Hilaire, St. Florent. Days & Hours: Mon.–Fri. 9–11:30, 2–6.

Et's. Lalanne E. & G., Tigne. Days & Hours: Mon.–Fri. 9–11:30, 2–6.

Et's. Touchais, Doué-la-Fontaine. Days & Hours: Mon.–Fri. 9–11:30, 2–6.

Et's. Verdier & Fils, Doué-la-Fontaine. Days & Hours: Mon.–Fri. 9–11:30, 2–6.

Et's. Robin & Co., Rablay sur Layon. Days & Hours: Mon.–Fri. 9–11:30, 2–6.

Vignobles & Caves de la Bouvraie, Ingandres sur Loire. Days & hours: Mon.–Fri. 9–11:30, 2–6.

Moc-Barie, Sté A. Besombres, Ackermann-Laurance, Veuve Amiot, Bouvet-Ladubay, Charbonneau-Lehou, De Neuville, Langlois-Château, all at St. Hilaire, St. Florent. Days & Hours: Mon.–Fri. 9–11:30, 2–6. (Also on Sat. and Sun. by appointment.) (Sparkling wines.)

Chapin-Landais, Chace. Days & Hours: Same as immediately above. (Sparkling wines.)

Gratien-Meyer & Seydoux, Beaulieu-les-Saumur. Days & Hours: Same as immediately above. (Sparkling wines).

Cooperative Agricole d'Ancenis, Ancenis (Loire-Atlantique).

Cooperative Vinicole de Brissac, Brissac. Days & Hours: Mon.–Fri. 9–11:30, 2–6.

Cooperative des Vignerons de Saumur, St. Cyr-en-Bourg. Days & Hours: Mon.–Fri. 9–11:30, 2–6.

Château de Serrant, Château de Savennières, Château de la Bizolière, Domaine de Chamboureau, all at Savennières, Coteaux de la Loire.

Château de Brissac, Cave Coopérative de Brissac, Brissac, Coteaux de l'Aubance.

Domaine d'Avrillé, Centre de dégustations, St. Jean des Mauvrets, Coteaux de l'Aubance.

Le Pic Martin, Centre de dégustations, *Château de l'Echarderie, Château de Belle-Rive, Château de la Guimonnière*, all at Rochefort sur Loire, Coteaux du Layon.

Château de la Roulerie, Domaine de l'Aiglerie, at Saint Aubin de Luigne, Coteaux du Layon.

Au Bon St. Lambert, Centre de dégustations, St. Lambert du Lattay.

La Promenade, Cave Coopérative La St. Vincent, Caveau du Vin, Jardins, all at Beaulieu sur Layon.

Domaine des Trottières at Thouarce.

Château de Fesles and *Château des Gauliers,* Bonneseaux-Thouarce.

Le Petit-Val, Chavagnes.

Château Montreuil-Bellay, Montsoreau, Saumur, Abbaye de Fontevrault, Saumur.

Château de Beauregard, Puy Notre Dame.

Clos des Murs and *Cave sous le Roc,* Parnay.

Château de Villeneuve, Souzay.

Caveau de dégustations, Concourson sur Layon.

BASSES ALPES

Syndicat des Producteurs de Vin de qualité des Basses Alpes, M. Jean D'Herbess, Domaine St. Jean, Manosque.

BORDEAUX

ADEB (Association pour le Développement de l'Exportation du Vin de Bordeaux), Maison du Vin, 1 Cours du xxx Juillet, Bordeaux. Tél.: 44.69.95.

Louis Eschenauer, S.A., 42 Avenue Emile Counord, Bordeaux. Days & Hours: Mon. afternoon–Fri. 9–11:30, 2:30–5. Arrangements should be made two days in advance of visit. Tour will include a visit to the plant, the caves where the wine is aged and the vineyards.

Dourthe Frères, Moulis-en-Médoc, Gironde. Days & Hours: Mon.–Fri. 8:30–12:30, 2:30–6. Advance notice: one day. Tour includes a visit to the plant, vineyards and Château of Médoc, wine tasting and samples.

Hanappier, Peyrelongue & Co., Ltd., 81 Cours du Médoc, Bordeaux. Days & Hours: Tues.–Thurs. 10–12, 3–5. Advance notice: one week.

Kressmann & Co., 72, Quai de Bacalan, Bordeaux. Days & Hours: Mon.–Fri. 8:30–12, 12:30–5:30. Write or telephone 24 hours in advance of visit.

Nathaniel Johnston & Fils, 93 Bis Quai Des Chartrons, Bordeaux.

Clossman & Co., 19–29 Rue Delord, Bordeaux.

Maison Albert Bichot, Beaune, Côte d'Or, and Bordeaux.

Sichel & Fils Frères, 80 Cours Balguerie–Stuttenberg, Bordeaux. Tel.: 294–128.

F. Ginestet, 133, Quai des Chartrons, Bordeaux.

Cruse & Fils Frères, 124 Quai Des Chartrons, Bordeaux, and Pommard, Côte d'Or.

Château Bottled Wines, Woltner Frères & Cie., 350 rue St. Honoré, Paris.

Et's. Vinicoles de Gironde. Gironde. Days & Hours: Tues.–Fri. 9–12, 2–5. Advance notice: 48 hours.

A.&R. Barrière Frères, 45, Cours du Médoc, Bordeaux. Days & Hours: Mon.–Fri. 9–11, 3–5. Advance notice: 48 hours. Tour will include a visit to the plant and the caves where the wine is aged.

Les Fils de Marcel Quancard, La Grave D'Ambares. Days & Hours: Daily except Sat. afternoon and Sundays. 9:00–5:30. Advance notice: two weeks.

G. Thellier (Plaine D'Antibes-R.N. 7) Commune De Villeneuve-Loubet.

A. de Luze & Fils, 88 Quai Des Chartrons, Bordeaux. Days: Mon.–Fri. Hours: By appointment. Telephone at least one day in advance of visit.

J. Calvet, 75 Cours du Médoc, Bordeaux. Days & Hours: Mon.–Fri. 9:30–12, 2:30–6. Advance notice: one day for groups of 5 or more. English speaking guide will conduct tour of plant and caves where the wine is aged.

Roger Joanne & Co., 40 Rue de Laseppe, Bordeaux. Days & Hours: Mon.–Fri. 9–11, 3–5. Advance notice: 24 hours.

Alexis Lichine & Co., Margaux (Gironde). Days & Hours: Mon.–Fri. 9–12, 2–6. Advance notice: 24 hours. Tour will include visits to the Château Prieure Lichine.

Barton and Guestier, 35 Cours Xavier-Arnozan, Bordeaux. Days & Hours: Tues.–Thurs. 2–4. Advance notice: 24 hours. Tour includes visiting the plant and the caves where the wine is aged.

Et's. Aurelien Grenouilleau, Sainte-Foy-la-Grande (Gironde). Days & Hours: Tues.–Fri. 9–7. Advance notice: 48 hours. The tour will include a visit to the plant and vineyard and tasting the various kinds of wines.

Chateau du Mayne (Sauternes), Barsac.

BURGUNDY

Bouchard Aine & Fils, Rue Ste.-Marguerite, Beaune. Days: Mon.–Fri.

Morin P. & F., Nuits-St.-Georges. Days & Hours: Daily. 9–12, 2–6. Same days and hours also for visits to the firm's Château de la Tour at Clos Vougeot, but the guide here (and on Sun. at Nuits-St.-Georges) does not speak English.

Geisweiler & Fils, Nuits-St.-Georges. Days: Mon.–Fri.

P. Bourée Fils, Gevrey-Chambertin. Daily visits.

F. Chauvenet, Nuits-St.-George, Côte d'Or.

Maison Louis Jadot, Beaune, Côte d'Or. Tel.: 129.

Champy Père & Cie., Beaune, Côte d'Or.

Chanson Père et Fils, Rue du College, Beaune, Côte d'Or.

Henri Gouges, Nuits-St.-Georges.

Marquis d'Angerville, Volnay.

E. Brocard & Fils, 22 Rue Richard, Beaune, Côte d'Or.

L'Heritier Guyot, 22 Rue de Longvic, Dijon.

Caves Exposition de la Reine Pedauque, Porte Saint Nicolas, Beaune.

Patriarche Pere et Fils, Beaune (Côte d'Or).

Simonnet-Febvre et Fils, Chablis.

CHAMPAGNE

Comité Interprofessionel du Vin de Champagne, 5 rue Henri Martin, Epernay.

Veuve Clicquot Ponsardin, 12 Rue du Temple, Reims. Phone: 47–33–60. Days & Hours: Mon.–Fri. 8:30–11, 2–4.

Victor Clicquot, 37 Rue du Champ de Mars, Reims. Phone: 47–31–67. Days & Hours: Mon.–Fri. 9–12, 2–5.

George Goulet, 2 Ave. General Giraud, Reims. Phone: 47–38–60. Days & Hours: Mon.–Fri. 8–12, 2–6.

Charles Heidsieck, 46 Rue de la Justice, Reims. Phone: 47–39–06.

Heidsieck & Co. Monopole, 83 Rue Coquebert, Reims. Phone: 47–39–34. Days & Hours: Mon.–Fri. 9–11, 2:30–4:30. Advance notice of arrival time and number in party.

Henriot, 22 Blvd. Diancourt, Reims. Phone: 47–25–23. Prefers visits in Nov. rather than Oct.

Ernest Irroy, 44 Blvd. Lundy, Reims. Phone: 47–13–67. Days & Hours: Mon.–Fri. 9–11, 2–4.

Lanson P. & F., 12 Blvd. Lundy, Reims. Phone: 47–59–71. Days & Hours: Mon.–Fri. 8–12, 2–5. Advance notice one month. Groups no larger than 10 people.

Veuve Laurent Perrier, Tours sur Marne. Phone: 6. Days & Hours: Mon.–Fri. 9–11, 2–4.

Mercier, 75 Ave. de Champagne, Epernay. Phone: 12–36. Every day including Sundays and holidays.

Maison Moët and Chandon, Epernay, or Maison Moët and Chandon, 7 Blvd. Malesherbes, Paris. Phone: Anjou 66–14. Epernay, Marne. Tel.: 971.

G. H. Mumm & Co., 29 Rue du Champ de Mars, Reims. Phone: 47–39–82. Days & Hours: Mon.–Fri. 9–11, 2–5.

P. Philipponnat & Co., Mareuil sur Ay. Phone: 12.

Rogeron, 70 à 82, rue Lesage, Reims.

Piper Heidsieck, 8 Rue Piper, Reims. Phone: 47–39–55. Days: Mon.–Fri.

Pommery & Greno, 131 Blvd. Pommesy, Reims. Phone: 47–29–51. Days & Hours: Mon.–Fri. 10–4.

Louis Roederer, 21 Blvd. Lundy, Reims. Phone: 47–59–81. Days: Mon.–Fri.

Ruinart P. & F., 4 Rue des Crayeres, Reims. Phone: 47–34–42. Days & Hours: Mon.–Fri. 9–12, 2–5.

Taittinger, 9 Place Saint Nicaise, Reims. Phone: 47–61–12. Every day, including Sundays and holidays: 8–12, 2–6.

J. Bollinger, Ay-Champagne, Marne.

COTES DE PROVENCE

Comité Régional de Propagande des Produits Agricoles de Provence et de Corse, 9 rue Montgrand, Marseille 6e.

La Commission De Propagande Du Comité Interprofessionel

Des Vins Côtes de Provence, Le Logis De Bonneau Villeneuve, Loubet (AM).

Ste. Domaine du Galoupet, Les Salins d'Hyères. Phone: 7. Daily visits. Advance notice by phone preferred.

Cooperative Mont Ste. Victoire, Puyloubier. Daily visits. Advance notice by phone preferred.

Cooperative l'Union, Pourcieux. Phone: 11. Daily visits. Advance notice by phone preferred.

Domaine de Montaud, Pierrefeu. Phone: 30. Daily visits. Advance notice by phone preferred after Nov. 1.

Château St. Martin, Taradeau. Phone: 1. Days & Hours: Daily. Advance notice by phone preferred. 8–12, 2–6.

Château Ste. Roseline Les Arcs, Les Arcs. Phone: 44. Daily visits. Advance notice by phone preferred.

Château des Vannieres, La Cadière d'Azur. Phone: 19. Daily visits. Advance notice required.

Domaine de Nestuby, Cotignac. Phone: 2. Daily visits. Advance notice required.

Domaine le Paradis, Le Luc. Days: Mon.–Tues. Advance notice required.

J. Isnard & Fils, 41 Rue Beaumont, Nice. Phone: 85–51–92. Days: Mon.–Tues. Advance notice required.

Et's. Bernard, Vidauban. Phone: 13. Daily visits. Advance notice required.

Château d'Aqueria, Tavel, Gard.

Syndicat des Producteurs de Vin A.O.C. de Palette par Aix (B.D.R.). Président: M. Rougier. Tél.: 31, Tholonet (B.D.R.)

Syndicat de Défense des Coteaux de Provence, Les Arcs par Draguignan, Var. Directeur: M. Corby. Tél.: 101.

Margnat Frères, 5 Quai de la Tourette, Marseille.

COTES DU RHONE

Wine Firms in the "Côtes du Rhône." Write to the Comité Interprofessional des Vins des Côtes du Rhône at Avignon for a complete list.

Syndicat de Défense des Producteurs de Vin des Côtes du Rhône, 92, Rue Joseph Vernet, Avignon, Vaucluse. Directeur: M. Ligier. Tél.: 81.24.64.

Paul Jaboulet Ainé, Tain l'Hermitage (Drôme).

SAONE-ET-LOIRE

Piat & Co., 23 Rue de la République, Macon.

TOURAINE

Et's. Bassereau, Vouvray.
Maison Bredif, Rochecorbon.
Et's. Foltz, Rochecorbon.
Maison Huet, Vouvray.
Et's. Turonia, 44 Route Nationale, Tours.
Maison Beauvilain, Chinon.
Et's. Monmousseau, Montrichard.
Et's. Bigot & Fils, Noyers.
Et's. Couly-Dutheil, Chinon.
Maison Audebert, Bourgueil.
Maison Dimpre, Bourgueil.

Vermouths, 190 *& Apéritifs*, 190

C.D.C.-Compagnie Générale des Produits Dubonnet, 30 avenue Kléber, Paris 16.

Noilly Prat & Cie, 165 rue Paradis, Marseille.

Société St-Raphael, 8 rue du Parc Royal, Paris 3e. Tél.: TUR 43–50. Hours: Afternoons Tues., Wed., Thurs.

Thibaud-Gaillard, Vinay (Isère).

Société Picon, 100 rue Paul Vaillant Courturier, Levallois-Perret. (Amer Picon, Pikina, Pec, Curacao Picon).

Cazalist & Prats, Sète, Hérault.

MONACO

Chocolates, 191

Caffarel Chocolate Factory. Arrangements should be made in advance of visit by writing to the *Monaco Information Center*, 630 Fifth Ave., N.Y. 20, N.Y.

GERMANY

Chocolates, 191

Frankonia, Schokoladenwerke Aktiengesellschaft, Würzburg. Tel.: 78501.

Cookies, 191

Bahlsen's Keksfabriken, Hannover.

Beer, 191

Erste Kulmbacher Actien-Brauerei, Kulmbach, Bayern.
Dinkelacker Brewery, Tuebingstr. 46, Stuttgart.
Holsten Brewery, Hamburg.
Löwenbräu Brewery, Nymphenburgerstrasse 4, Munich. Guided tours, Mon.–Fri.
Paulaner–Salvator Thomasbrau A. G., München.
Würzburger Hofbrau A.G., Würzburg.

Brandy, 192

VERBAND DER MARKENSPIRITUOSEN-
INDUSTRIE e.V.

Asbach-Uralt, Rüdesheim am Rhine. Visitors can join a con-
ducted tour through Asbach distillery and receive a free
sample of brandy.

Bommerlunder und Balle Vertrieb, Herm. G. Dethleffsen,
Schliessfach 365, Flensburg.

Doornkaat Aktiengesellschaft, Norden/Ostfriesland.

Dujardin & Co., vorm. Gebr. Melcher Postfach 106, Krefeld–
Uerdingen/Rh.

Weinbrennerei Peter Eckes, Nieder–Olm b.Mainz.

H. C. König Markenvertrieb, Steinhagen/Westf.

Anton Riemerschmid, Weinbrennerei und Likörfabrik, Pra-
terinsel 3, München 22.

Weinbrennerei Scharlachberg, Bingen/Rhein.

H. W. Schlichte, Steinhagen/Westf.

Mampe Hamburg, Eiffestr. 600–604, Hamburg 26.

Teucke & Koenig Co., Hannover.

Wines, 192–193

VERBAND DEUTSCHER SEKTKELLEREIEN e.V.

Burgeff & Co. A.-G., Wiesbadenstr. 1, Hochheim/Main.

Deinhard & Co. oHG., Deinhard Platz, Koblenz.

Henkell & Co. K.G., Henkellsfeld, Wiesbaden-Biebrich.

G. C. Kessler & Co., Esslingen.

Chr. Adt. Kupferberg, Kupferbergstr. 17, Mainz/Rhein.

Matheus Müller K.G. A.A., Matheus Müller-Platz 1, Eltville/
Rhein.

Söhnlein Rheingold K.G., Wilhelmstr. 1–3, Wiesbaden-
Schierstein.

Wines

A. Steigenberger, Hainerweg 37–53, Frankfurt am Main.

M. Meyer (Rhine & Moselle Wines) Rüdesheim am Rhein.

Weinkellerei Carl Reh KG., Leiwen/Mosel.

Vereinshaus Treviris AG., Trier/Mosel.

Weinkellerei Scholl & Hillebrand, Rüdesheim/Rheingau.

Weinkellerei Franz Winkel KG., Oestrich/Rheingau.

Schulz & Wagner, Postcheck FFM 345 Frankfurt/M.

Wein- u. Sektkellerei Langenbach & Co., Worms.

Weinkellerei P.J., Worms/Rheinhessen.

Weingut Heinrich Lorch, Bergzabern/Weinstrasse.

Weinkellierei Hellmut Baumann & Co., Frankfurt/Main.

Reichsgräflich von Plettenberg'sche Weinkellereiverwaltung, Bad Kreuznach/Nahe.

Weingut Louis Guntrum, Rheinallee Nr. 63, Nierstein am Rhein, Tel: Oppenheim 707.

Sichelonia Weinexport GmbH., Kaiserstrasse 26–30, Mainz, Tel: 2–4678.

Friedr. Carl Ott & Co., Frankenweinkellerei, Würzburg.

Anheuser & Fehrs, Bruckes 41, Bad Kreuznach.

Richard Langguth, Traben–Trarbach a.d. Mosel. Tel: 221.

Messrs. Wilh. Wasum, Bacharach am Rhein.

Reichsgraf Von Kesselstatt, Hauptverwaltung, Trier/Mosel.

Pfortenhaus, Kloster Eberbach/Rhg.

Deinhard & Co., Koblenz an Rhein und Mosel.

Julius Kayser & Co., Traben-Trarbach.

BELGIUM

Endive

Belgian Endive Association, c/o Office National des De-
bouches Agricoles et Horticoles, Mr. A. Vandendael, Director General, 7, Rue Gaucheret, Brussels. N.Y.

Hotel Training Schools

C.E.R.I.A. (Centre d'Etudes et de Recherches de l'Industrie
Alimentaire), Avenue Emile Gryson, Anderlecht (Bruxelles). Directeur: M. Doms.

Ecole Professionnelle Communale d'Hôtellerie, 13, Rue Hors-
Château, Liége. Directeur: M. Dubois.

Ecole Professionnelle Provinciale d'Industrie Hôtelière, Rue
Saint-Donat, Namur. Directeur: M. Denayer.

Ecole Hôtelière Spermalie, 7, Snaggaardstraat, Bruges. Directeur: M. le Chanoine Van de Stiettele.

Hotelierschool, Massartstraat, 8, Koksijde. Directeur: Eer-
waarde Heer Avonture.

Stedelijk Instituut, 1, Leopold de IIIde laan, Oostende. Directeur: M. Decleyre.

LUXEMBOURG

Breweries

Brasserie de Luxembourg, Luxembourg-Clausen.
Brasserie Funck-Bricher, Luxembourg-Grund.
Brasserie Henri Funck, Luxembourg-Neudorf.

Wines

Caves coopératives de Wellenstein, Wellenstein.
Caves St. Martin, Remich.
Caves coopératives des vignerons, Wormeldange.
Caves coopératives des vignerons, Grevenmacher.

~~~~~~

NETHERLANDS

~~~~~~

Beer

Heineken's Brewery, Amsterdam.
Heineken's Export Brewery, Rotterdam. Days & Hours:
   Mon.–Fri. 10–12, 2–4. Telephone for appointment.
Amstel Brewery, Mauritskade 14, Amsterdam. Days & Hours:
   Mon.–Fri. 10–2. Tel.: 5–9711.

Candy

Sagitta Factory (Fruit Drop Rolls), Amsterdam.
Van Melle N.V., Olympiaweg 10, Rotterdam.

Dairy Products

De Sierkan, Lulofstraat 20–30, The Hague. Tel.: 111906.
   Visits: Mon.–Fri. 9–11:30, inspection of milking machinery.
   Group maximum 40. By appointment.
Coöp. Fabriek van Melkproducten "Aurora," Opmeer. Tel.:
   301. Visits: 9–10. Two-hour tour. By appointment.
Fa. Jac Wiedemeijer & Zn., De Erven 22, Broek in Water-
   land. Visits: 9–6 daily.

Food-Stuffs

P. de Gruyter & Zoon N.V., Orthenstraat 16, 's-Hertogen-bosch. Visits: Mon.–Fri. By appointment.

Erven de Wed. (Coffee, tobacco), J. v. Nelle, N.V., Rotter-dam. Mon.–Fri. Appointments by mail.

N.V. Lubro (Bread), Hogenoord 1, Utrecht. Tel.: 11851. Visits: One-hour tour. By telephone appointment.

Spirits

N.V. Erven Lucas Bols, Rozengracht 103, Amsterdam. Museum hours: Mon.–Fri. 10–12, 2–4.

N. V. Likeurstokerij, Wijnand Fockink, O.Z. Voorburgwal, Amsterdam. Tel.: 232234.

P. Melchers (De Locomotief), Langehaven 74–76, Schiedam. Tel.: 67510. Collection of miniature bottles with more than 5000 liquors from all over the world. Visits: Appointment several days in advance. Groups must state size.

DENMARK

Beer

Carlsberg Brewery, 100 Vester Faelledvej, Copenhagen. All guided tours. Special appointments by phone (Central 7000 —Ext. 292).

Tuborg Brewery, Strandvej 54, Copenhagen.

Spirits

AQUAVIT

Danish Distilleries, Aalborg, Jutland.

LIQUEUR

Peter F. Heering Distilleries, Over Gaden neden Vandet, 11, Copenhagen.

Cherry Wine Producers of Denmark Ltd., Hestemollestraede 6, Copenhagen.

J. J. Jacobsen & Co. (Cherry Bestle), 11 Sankt Anna Plads, Copenhagen.

SWEDEN

Beer

St. Erik's Brewery, Kungsgatan 19, Stockholm.

A/B Pripp & Lyckholm, Stampgatan 18, Gothenburg, C.

A/B Stockholms Bryggerier (Stockholm's Breweries Ltd.), Stockholm.

A/B Malmö Forenade Bryggerier, Lantmannagatan 59, Malmo. N.Y. Rep.: *Swedish Beer Export Division of G. L. Beijer of Sweden*, Mr. Anders P. Larson, Mgr., 642 Chrysler Bldg., N.Y.C.

Canned Foods

Findus, Sundbyberg, Malmö. Very modern methods employed. Vegetables are canned in the fields immediately after being picked.

Chocolates

Marabou Chocolate Factory, Sundbyberg, Stockholm.

Food

Olson Trading Co., 1 Pondfield Rd., Bronxville, N.Y. Write for information about visiting Swedish food factories.

FINLAND

[Arrangements should be made in advance of visit to Jalostaja, Fincos, Leiras and Marli by writing to *Mr. Erkki Railo*, Export Manager, Huhtamakiyhtyma Oy, Kaisaniemenkatu 6, Helsinki.]

Foods

BREADS, BISCUITS, WAFERS, MACARONI

†*Ipnos Factory*, Huhtamakiyhtyma Oy, Turku 17. Days & Hours: Mon.–Fri. 10–1.

CHEESE

Valio Meijerien Keskusosuusliike, Kalevank 61, Helsinki. U.S. Rep.: *Atalanta Trading Co.*, 77 Hudson St., N.Y.C.

CHOCOLATES, CONFECTIONS, CANDY, BISCUITS

†*Hellas Factory*, Huhtamakiyhtyma Oy, Turku 17. Days & Hours: Mon.–Fri. 10–1.

†*Karl Fazer, Inc.*, Fabriksgatan 29, Helsinki. A written notice

† Represented in U.S. by *Finn Foods, Inc.*, 114 E Main St., Bogota, N.J.

should be given 2-3 weeks prior to visit. U.S. Rep.: *Mr. Louis P. Alaimo,* 50 Kinderkamack Road, Oradell, N.J.

JUICES, JAMS, PRESERVES, CANNED AND FROZEN
GOODS

†*Jalostaja Factory.*

Wines, Champagne, Liqueurs, Soft Drinks, Ice Cream

†*Marli Factory.*

† Represented in U.S. by *Finn Foods, Inc.,* 114 E Main St., Bogata, N.J.

NORWAY

Beer

Ringnes Brewery, Thv Meyersgate 2, Oslo. Tel.: 37-18-00. Mr. Harald Maartman, export manager. Write in advance or telephone day before visit.

Frydenlund Brewery, Pilestredet 52, Oslo, Tel.: 46-38-00.

Schous Brewery, Trondheimsveien 2, Oslo, Tel.: 42-63-00.

Cheese

O *Kavli Cheese Factory,* Damsgårdsvei 59, Bergen. Tel.: 98-0-40. Producers of *Primula* and other kinds of packaged cheeses.

Farming

Norway's Agricultural College. Famous for scientific research projects. Situated at As, 26 miles from Oslo (1 hr. by train).

Write in advance to *Norges Landbrukshogskole*, Vollebekk. Tel.: As 9200.

Stabburet Canning Factory (Fish, meat, vegetables) in Fredrikstad, small town 2 hours' drive south of Oslo on east side of the Oslo Fjord, welcomes visitors *from 1964* when the new factory building is completed. Fredrikstad. Tel.: 5831.

Fish

Fish Canning Industry, Stavanger. Write in advance to *Stavanger Travel Association*, Kongsgate 10, Stavanger. Tel.: 2–84–37.

Stavanger on the south-west coast of Norway is the headquarters for the Norwegian canning industry (fish, sardines), and there is also to be found a canning laboratory and a canning high school.

Outstanding attractions in the same field: the fish markets in Bergen and Stavanger.

IRELAND

Beer

Cherry's Breweries Ltd., Waterford. Tel.: Waterford 4963.

Guinness Brewery, St. James Gate, Dublin. Hours: Special guides conduct visitors on weekdays between 10 and 3, and on Saturday at 10.

E. Smithwick & Sons Ltd., Kilkenny, Co. Kilkenny. Tel.: Kilkenny 14.

Biscuits

W. R. Jacob & Co., Ltd., Dublin. Hours: Weekdays, 11:15 a.m.; 3 p.m. (1½ hour tour.) Appointments should be made one day in advance by phoning sales office: Dublin 5-3351.

Liqueur

Irish Mist Liqueur Co., Tullamore. N.Y. Rep.: *Munson G. Shaw Co., Inc.*, 400 Madison Ave., N.Y. 17, N.Y. Hours: Mon.–Fri. 10–4.

Stout

Beamish & Crawford Ltd., South Moln St., Cork. Tel.: Cork 20001.

Guinness & Son Co. Ltd., St. James' Gate Brewery, Dublin. Tel.: 56701.

Whiskey

Cork Distilleries Co. Ltd. (Paddy, Murphy), Morrisons Island, Cork. Tel.: Cork 23106.

Gilbeys of Ireland Ltd. (Crock of Gold), Upper O'Connell St., Dublin. Tel.: 40641.

Irish Distillers Ltd. (Dunphy's Original Irish), 2 Lr. Merrion St., Dublin. Tel.: 65084.

John Jameson & Son Ltd. (John Jameson), Bow St. Distillery, Dublin. Tel.: 76748.

John Power & Son Ltd. (Powers Gold Label), John's Lane Distillery, Dublin. Tel.: 76748.

D. E. Williams Ltd. (Tullamore Dew), Tullamore, Co. Offaly. Tel.: Tullamore 9.

Wines

FRUIT WINE

Vineyard Products Co. Ltd., Seville Place, Dublin. Tel.: 49088.

PRUNE WINE

Wm. & P. Thompson Ltd., Gardiner St., Dublin. Tel.: 79409.

AUSTRIA

[Arrangements should be made in advance of visit by writing directly to the Austrian State Tourist Department, 444 Madison Avenue, New York 22, N.Y.

Beer

Schwechat Brewery, Landstrasser Hauptstrasse 97, Vienna 3.

Cheese

Tiroler Sennereiverband, Brixnerstrasse 1, Innsbruck.
Franz Tollinger, Sillhofe, Innsbruck.
Max Klausner, St. Johann/Tirol, Tyrol.
Alfons Tunner, Viaduktbogen 136–39, Innsbruck.
Tiroler Glashutte, Claus Josef Riedel, KG., Kufstein, Tyrol.

Mineral Waters

Bottling Plant. Sulz, near Güssing, Burgenland Province.

Tobacco

Tabakfabrik, Untere Donaulände, Linz on Danube.

Wines

(Wine Cellar) Sepp Hoeld, St. Georgen, Burgenland.
Vintner Association, St. Margarethen, Burgenland.

ITALY

Chocolates

Perugina, Perugia. For information: International Buitoni Perugia, Via Nizza 142, Rome. Tel.: 848.467.

Pasta

Buitoni, Sansepolcro (Arezzo). For information: International Buitoni Perugia, Via Nizza 142, Rome. Tel.: 848.467.

Wines

Messrs. Francesco Bertolli, Lucca. Days & Hours: Mon.–Fri. 10–4.

Marchesi Lodovico E/ Piero Antinori, Palazzo Antinori, Piazza Antinori, Florence. Tel.: 2–8298.

Ditta P. Caruso, Casa Vinicola, Ravello (Salerno). Tel.: 11.

Diego Rallo & Figli (Marsala), Via Sebastiano Lipari, 8, Marsala. Tel.: 1037.

Cantine Aurora (Verdicchio), Casella Postale, 8, Cupramontana (Ancona). Tel.: 311–236–335.

Di Prospero (Abruzzo) Bagnaturo Di Pratola Peligna (L'Aquila). Tel.: 21395.

Terme di Montecatini (Montecatini Waters), Viale Verdi, 41, Montecatini Terme. Tel.: 26–51.

Fratelli Sterzi (Veronese Wines, Bardolino, etc.), San Martino B.A., Verona. Tel.: 39.

G. B. Pezziol (VOV, Zabajone & CYNAR Aperitif Wines), Via A. Pertile, 49, Padova. Tel.: 20.062

S. A. Chianti Ruffino, Via Corsica 12, Casella Postale 305, Brescia. Tel.: 58042.

Casa Vinicola Suali (Chianti) Via Bonifacio Lupi 14, Florence. Tel.: 45013.

La Carretta (Piedmontese Wines), Piobesi d'Alba.

Cantine Soc. di Marino (Marino & Frascati), Viale del Lavoro, Ciampino (Marino). Tel.: 692.001.

Guglielmo Zuccotti (Ligurian Wines, Portofino), Via G. Mazzini, Rapallo. Tel.: 50.587.

Marcello Cirillo-Farrusi (Puglie Wines), Tenuta Casa al Quarto Cerignola. Tel.: 3–28.

Campari Export-Import (Bitter Campari L'Aperitivo), Via Manzoni 19, Milano.

Gancia & Cia, Canelli (Asti). Tel.: 81.121.

Flli. Ferrero (Vermouth), Via Magenta, 14, Torino. Tel.: 528–246/7/3/9.

Giacomo Borgogno (Piedmontese Wines), Barolo. Tel.: 4–8.

Petrurbani (Orvieto), Casella Postale, 82, Orvieto.

Scala (Grande Marche Assoc.) (Campanian Wines, Capri, Lacrima Christi), Via Sardegna, 50, Rome. Tel.: 20.062.

Luigi Bosca (Sparkling Wines), Canelli (Asti). Tel.: 81.161.

E. Isolabella & Figlio (Fior D'Alpe), Via Cimarosa 14, Milano.

Casa Vinicola Barone Ricasoli (Chianti), 7 Via Maggio, Florence. Tel.: 270.808.

PORTUGAL

Canned Fish

Algarve Exportador, Lda., Matosinhos.
Fab. de Conservas Vasco da Gama, Matosinhos.
Fab. de Conservas Vasco da Gama, Setubal.
Marques, Neves Ca., Lda., Matosinhos.
Marques, Neves and Ca., Lda., Portimao.

Wines

Gremio dos Exportadores de Vinho do Porto, Palacio da Associação, Rua de Ferreira Borges, Porto. Tel.: 25191-2-3.
Cockburn Ports, Oporto. Days & Hours: Mon.–Fri. 10–4.
Richard Hooper & Sons, Vila Nova De Gaia.
Jose Maria da Fonseca, Largo do Corpo Santo, 6-2.°, Lisbon.
Messias Baptista, Mealhada.
Sogrape, R. Firmeza, 487, Oporto.
Real Vinicola Vinicola de Norte de Portugal, Vila Nova de Gaia.
Roberston Bros. & Co. Ltd., Rua Dr. Antonio, Vila Nova de Gaia.
Feuerheerd Bros. & Co., Ltd., Rua Serpa Pinto, 490 Villa Nova de Gaia, Oporto.
Cockburn Smithes & Co., Vila Nova de Gaia.
Silva & Cosens Ltd., Vila Nova de Gaia. Tel.: Oporto 710171.
Leacock & Co., Funchal, Madeira.

SPAIN

Wines

Fernando A. de Terry, S.A., P.O. Box 30, Puerto de Santa Maria.

Duff Gordon & Company, Puerto de Santa Maria, Andalucia.

Vinicola Hidalgo & Cia., S.A., Sanlucar de Barrameda. P.O. Box 22.

Williams & Humbert, Ltd., Apartado de Lorreos No. 23, Jerez de la Frontera.

Gonzalez Byass & Co., Ltd., Jerez de la Frontera.

Jose Romero P. Gil, San Juan de Dios 13, Jerez de la Frontera.

Bodegas Bilbainas, S.A., P.O. Box 124, Bilbao.

Bosch & Cia, P.O. Box 475, Barcelona.

Lopez Hermanos, P.O. Box 51, Malaga.

Luis Caballero, S.A., Federico Rubio No. 93. Tel.: 1300.

Manuel Fernandez y Cia, S.L., or *Bobadilla y Cia*, Cristal 4. Tel.: 41863.

Palomino & Vergara, S.A., Calle Colón 1/25. Tel.: 41883.

Jose Pemartin & Cia, S.A., Pizarro No. 17. Tel.: 41395 and 41497.

Sandeman Bros. & Co., Calle Pizarro. Tel.: 41892–3.

Wisdom & Warter Ltd., Pizarro 7. Tel.: 41007.

Pedro Domecq, S.A., San Ildefonso, 3. Tel.: 41800.

Bodegas Rioja Santiago, Haro-Rioja Alta.

Garvey, S.A., Bodegas de San Patricio Guadalete, 14.

SWITZERLAND

Beer

Actienbrauerei Basel, Basel.

P. Bartenstein AG, Brauerei Uster, Uster ZH.

Beauregard SA, Fribourg.

Beretta SA, Birreria Nazionale, Locarno.

Bierbrauerei Langenthal, Langenthal.

Bierbrauerei Schützengarten AG, St. Gallen.

Bierbrauerei Steinhölzli AG, Bern.

Birra Bellinzona SA, Bellinzona.

Brasserie Valaisanne SA, Sion.

Brauerei Falken AG, Schaffhausen.

Brauerei Feldschlösschen, Rheinfelden.

Brauerei Felsenau AG, Bern.

Brauerei zum Gurten AG, Bern.

Brauerei Haldengut AG, Winterthur.

Brauerei A. Hürlimann AG, Zürich.

Brauerei Wädenswil, Weber & Cie., Wädenswil ZH.

Brauerei Warteck AG, Basel.

Brasserie du Cardinal, Fribourg.

Comète SA, La Chaux-de-Fonds.

Fertig Frères SA, Brasserie d'Orbe, Orbe VD.

Hofweber & Co. AG, Zollikofen-Bern.

Löwenbräu Zürich AG, Zürich.

Luzerner Brauerei zum Eichhof AG, Luzern.

Müller SA Brasserie, Neuchâtel.

H. Müller AG, Brauerei, Baden.

Nessi & Ci., Lugano.

Rhätische Aktien-Brauereien, Chur.

Salmenbräu Rheinfelden AG, Rheinfelden.

Cheese

[The following establishments, near Berne, are included in the *Switzerland Cheese Association* tour.]

Cheese factory in either Jegenstorf or Krauchthal.

Cheese cellar of an exporter in Burgdorf.

Swiss Cheese Union's Prepacking Plant "Swisspack" in Burgdorf.

Day: Tues., beginning Oct. 2 and ending Nov. 27.

Hours: 8–12.

Tourists are to call the *Swiss Cheese Union, Inc.* in Berne (Tel. No. 45–33–31) one day, or more, in advance, to inform the Swiss Cheese Union of their visit and to enable the head office to arrange for transportation, etc.

Chocolates

Tobler Chocolate, Berne. Days & Hours: Mon.–Thurs. 9–2:30.

Spirits

Etter et Fils, Zug.

Arnold Dettling, Brunnen. Tél.: (043) 9 17 68.

Basler Kirschwasser (Rum Company Ltd.), 141–145 Gueterstrasse, Basle.

Wines

VAUD

Hammel S. A., Rolle.

Louis Bovard S. A., Cully.

Henri Badoux, Aigle.

J. & P. Testuz, Treytorrens-Cully.

Cave de La Côte, Morges.

VALAIS

Hoirs Charles Bonvin Fils, Sion.
Hoirs L. Imesch, Sierre.
Hoirs Frédéric Varone, Sion.
Albert Biollaz & Cie, Saint-Pierre-de-Clages.
Provins, Sion.

NEUCHATEL

S. A. Samuel Châtenay, Neuchâtel.
Domaine E. de Montmollin Fils, Auvernier.
Domaine Philippe Coste, Auvernier.

TESSIN

Cantina sociale del Mendrisiotto, Mendrisio.

LUCERNE

Léo Wunderle A. G., Luzern.

LAUSANNE

Société des Exportateurs de Vins Suisses, Bellefontaine 18,
Lausanne.

GREAT BRITAIN

Biscuits

Huntley & Palmer, Ltd., Reading, Berkshire. Address Visi-
tors' Reception Department.
Peek, Frean & Co. Ltd., Keetons Road, Bermondsey, London.
Tel.: BERmondsey 3521.

Breweries

Brewers' Society, 42 Portman Square, London, W.1. Tel.: WELbeck 0382.

Charrington & Co. Ltd., Anchor Brewery, Mile End, London E.1. Tel.: Stepney Green 1860.

Guinness Exports Ltd., 8, Baker Street, London W.1. Tel.: WELbeck 9101.

Caterers

J. S. Lyons & Co. Ltd., Cadby Hall, London W.14. Tel.: RIVerside 2040.

Cheese

The Cooperative Wholesale Society, Ltd. (Cheddar and Cheshire), Melin Rug, Corwen, Merioneth, North Wales; Llandyrnog, near Denbigh, North Wales. Address the Production Manager, Milk Products Department, Beechgrove, London Road, Cirencester, Gloucestershire.

T. G. W. Wiles (Stilton Cheese), Long Clowson, near Melton Mowbray.

J. M. Nuttall & Co., Ltd. (Stilton, Derbyshire, and Leicestershire), Dove Dairy, Hartington, near Buxton, Derbyshire. Address the Manager, Mr. A. Williamson.

The following large creameries between them manufacture Stilton, Double Gloucester, Derby, Caerphilly, Wensleydale, Lancashire, Leicester, Cheshire and Cheddar cheese:

Wilts. United Dairies, Trowbridge, Wiltshire. Address Mr. F. M. Featherstone.

Whitelock's Ltd., 24 Tynedale Street, Stockton on Tees, Co. Durham. Address Mr. A. W. Austin.

Express Dairy Foods Ltd., 2–10 Commonside East, Mitcham, Surrey. Address Mr. F. A. Grantham.

Milk Marketing Board (Cheddar, Coloured and White Cheshire, Caerphilly, Double Gloucester), Thames Ditton, Surrey. Address Mr. T. H. Hollins.

Chocolates

Carsons Ltd. (Liqueur Chocolates), Bristol. Address Mr. A. Eastman, Marketing Director.

Cadbury's Chocolates, Bourneville, Birmingham.

J. S. Fry & Sons, Ltd., Somerdale, Bristol. Address Mr. M. Tugwell.

Cider & Mead, etc.

The Mead House, Gulval, Mount's Bay, Cornwall. The ancient drink is made, bottled and sold for consumption on the premises.

Rose's Lime Juice, 1–6 Connaught Place, London W.2.

Whiteways Cider Co. Ltd., The Orchards, Whimple, Exeter, Devon.

Spirits

ENGLAND

James Burrough, Ltd. (Gin), Beefeater House, Hutton Road, London S.E. 11. Tel.: RELiance 3301.

Lemon Hart & Son, Ltd. (Rum), 40 Eastcheap, London, E.C. 3.

H. D. Davies & Co., Ltd. (Pimm's), 98–100 Bishopsgate London E.C. 2.

Coates & Co., Ltd., Black Friars Distillery, 59 & 60 Southside Street, Plymouth, Devon. Address Mr. R. T. Harris. Tel.: 65292.

Scotch Whiskey Association, 30 Bruton Street, London W.I. Tel.: MAYfair 4384.

SCOTLAND

William Grant & Sons, Ltd., 206–208 West George Street, Glasgow C-2.

Wm. Teacher & Sons, Ltd., 14 St. Enoch Square, Glasgow C. 1. Tel.: CENtral 7564.

Peter Dawson Ltd. 133 Waterloo Street, Glasgow, C.2.

Chivas Brothers, Ltd. 20 Renfield Street, Glasgow. Tel.: CENtral 0217.

Bulloch Lade & Co. Ltd., 133 Waterloo Street, Glasgow C.2.

John Robertson & Son, Ltd., 10 Links Place, Leith, Edinburgh 6. Tel.: LEIth 3216–9.

Scottish Malt Distillers, Ltd., 15 Coates Crescent, Edinburgh, 3. Tel.: CALedonian 6202.

Scotch Whiskey Association, 77 George Street, Edinburgh, 2.

James & George Stodart Ltd., Old Smuggler, Dumbarton. Tel.: DUMbarton 600.

White Horse Distillers Ltd., 120 St. Vincent Street, Glasgow C.2.

Teas

Brooke Bond & Co., Ltd., 35 Cannon Street, London, E.C. 4, one of Britain's biggest blenders and packers, will receive visitors seriously interested in tea and perhaps arrange for them to visit a teatasting in Mincing Lane. Telephone in advance Mr. G. W. Powell, CITy 6422.

R. Twining & Co., Ltd., Ibex House, Minories, London, E.C. 3. Founded 1706. Contact Mr. H. R. Hughes, one of the Directors, or in his absence, Mr. C. A. L. Circuitt, the Export Manager.

Wines

Williams & Humbert, Ltd., Sherry House, 39 Crutched Friars, London E.C. 3.

Gonzalez Byass & Co., Ltd., 91 Park Street, London W 1.

Geo. G. Sandeman Sons & Co. Ltd., 20 St. Swithin's Lane, London E.C. 4.

John Harvey & Sons Ltd., Harvey House, 12 Denmark Street, Bristol 1. Tel.: Bristol 2–7661.

Index